God and Race in American Politics

MARK A. NOLL

God and Race in American Politics

A Short History

PRINCETON UNIVERSITY PRESS

PRINCETON AND OXFORD

Copyright © 2008 by Princeton University Press
Published by Princeton University Press,
41 William Street, Princeton, New Jersey 08540

In the United Kingdom: Princeton University Press, 6 Oxford Street,
Woodstock, Oxfordshire OX20 1TW

Library of Congress Cataloging-in-Publication Data

Noll, Mark A., 1946–
God and race in American politics : a short history / Mark A. Noll.
p.   cm.
Includes bibliographical references and index.
ISBN 978-0-691-12536-7 (hardcover : alk. paper)
1. United States—Race relations—Political aspects.   2. Christianity and
politics—United States—History.   3. African Americans—Civil rights—
History.   4. African Americans—Religion.   5. African Americans—
Intellectual life.   6. United States—Politics and government—19th
century.   7. United States—Politics and government—20th century.
8. United States—Politics and government—2001–.   I. Title.
E185.N65   2008
305.800973—dc22   2008016456

British Library Cataloging-in-Publication Data is available

This book has been composed in Janson
Printed on acid-free paper. ∞
press.princeton.edu

Printed in the United States of America

1   3   5   7   9   10   8   6   4   2

To

David and Bethany

Contents

Illustrations

Acknowledgments

This book is a revision and expansion of the Stafford Little Lectures that were presented at Princeton University on October 17, 18, and 19, 2006. For the invitation to offer these lectures, I am most grateful to the Princeton Lecture Committee and Princeton University Press. Fred Appel of the Press has been a most encouraging (and editorially discerning) promoter of this project. At Princeton, Robert Wuthnow, Leigh Eric Schmidt, and R. Marie Griffith were unusually gracious hosts, and I also benefited from a stimulating discussion organized by David Michelson, acting associate director of Princeton's Center for the Study of Religion. To those who attended the lectures, I offer my thanks for insightful comments and probing questions that led me to expand or modify here some of what was first presented there.

I would like to thank Ethan Sanders, Darren Grem, Rusty Hawkins, Jeremy Wells, Christopher Luse, and Bryan Bademan for assisting with research in various ways. David Chappell, Dennis Dickerson, and Thabiti Anyabwile had nothing to do with the manuscript directly, but their own work and their responses to a few key questions were critical for what I have attempted. To Luke Harlow, John McGreevy, Ed Blum, and the Press's two anonymous readers

I am very grateful for many helpful suggestions. I also owe a large and long-standing debt to Bud Kellstedt for many conversations on the themes of this book, and to Bud and his colleagues John Green, Jim Guth, and Corwin Smidt for their careful counting of votes in relationship to religious beliefs, behavior, and adherence. Work on this project was also crucially assisted by the Cary and Ann Maguire Fellowship in Ethics and American History of the Kluge Center at the Library of Congress, the history department of Wheaton College, and the history department of the University of Notre Dame.

Finally, it is a pleasure to thank family members for their aid along the way: Robert Noll, who did the graphs; David Noll, who consulted on Supreme Court decisions; and especially Maggie Noll, who has provided self-sacrificing support for my writing life that goes back a very long time and that has been especially appreciated in recent hectic days. The dedication, which is first for love, expresses great admiration as well.

God and Race in American Politics

Introduction

This book offers a simply stated thesis about an immensely complicated history. First, race has always been among the most influential elements in American political history, and in many periods absolutely the most influential. Second, religion has always been crucial for the workings of race in American politics. Together, race and religion make up, not only the nation's deepest and most enduring moral problem, but also its broadest and most enduring political influence.

Yet *how* race and religion have interacted to shape politics has differed dramatically over time and by community. Before the Civil War, religion drove abolitionist assaults upon slavery even as it undergirded influential defenses of slavery in both the North and the South. After that conflict, religion and politics worked very differently for African Americans than for the white majority culture. On the one side, church life opened a limited space for black social organization and intellectual improvement, even though the political effects of that opening would not be evident for another century. On the other side, the political effects were immediate. A Christianity mostly bereft of its antebellum social vitality played a major part in sanctioning systematic white discrimination against African Americans. In turn, the racially defined polity that religious forces helped to create became a fixed reality of American politics into the 1960s and a precipitate of much political change thereafter. For the recent past, complexity continues. African-American religion helped spark the civil rights movement that left immense political and cultural changes in its wake, but the broader effects of that movement also keyed a politically conservative countermovement inspired by a different kind of religion. The political realignments of the last forty years, which are the most thorough of such realignments in American history, were by no means caused by religion alone, but religious factors have been everywhere evident in their development.

In other words, rather than any specific configuration of race and religion, it has been the general interweaving of race with religion, along with a discernibly religious mode of public argument, that have pervaded the nation's political history. The religious note in American political discourse has been a source of foreign comment from before de Tocqueville to the present.[1] It is rooted in the United States' broadly Calvinist-evangelical heritage that bequeathed a style of public discourse that continues to exert great influence, even for many who have passed far beyond the religious convictions of earlier Americans. An earnest moral concern for how governments should conduct themselves, a compulsion to sermonize about the duties of citizens and the state, and a frequent recourse to Scripture for grounding or garnishing political positions have been consistently present in American history, from nineteenth-century debates over slavery, war, and Reconstruction to recent controversies over civil rights, economic opportunity, right to life, and the ordering of families.

No short history can fully encompass such complicated themes and such complex events, but it does possess the advantage of portraying different American eras as parts of a continuous story. In addition, a short history may allow for a sharper understanding of how interconnections among politics, race, and religion have developed over time than can be provided by the detailed studies of individual periods and events that I have relied upon so gratefully in putting together this synthesis.

There are, alas, any number of incidents, statements, or situations that could be used to introduce this kind of history—although "alas" is far too simple an interjection for the complexities of the story from Nat Turner to George W. Bush. To treat broad and weighty subjects in short compass means that I will be presenting something more like a cartoon than a real history. But even cartoons can offer a few moments of sharp focus.

One such moment occurred in July 1863, the climactic month of the nation's most enduringly significant crisis. Earlier in July, crucial victories at Gettysburg and Vicksburg turned the military tide of the Civil War in favor of the North; a week later federal officials in New York City began to carry out the draft that Congress had authorized in order to meet the war's escalating demands for manpower. On Saturday, July 18, Sgt. Robert Simmons, an African American from New York City who had enlisted in the Fifty-fourth Massachusetts Regiment of Col. Robert Gould Shaw, was killed during the Union assault on Fort Wagner, South Carolina. His death occurred only days after antidraft rioters in New York City, hell-bent on attacking the city's Negro population, had destroyed Simmons's family home and lynched his nephew. The riots, as a protest against the draft in general and especially the provision that allowed men of means to hire a substitute, were fueled by the rage of poor white immigrants and left hundreds of African Americans dead. The day before Robert Simmons's death in far-away South Carolina, Maria Daly, a white diarist, had expressed fears that the New York mob would attack the block in which her home was located, since it was situated near tenements below MacDougal Street, where a band of African Americans had taken refuge on a rooftop. On that rooftop this black contingent was collecting firearms for self-defense and singing psalms for divine protection.[2]

Only a few years later, a conservative Catholic periodical in Munich published a long article by Father Paul Joseph Münz on the subject "Christendom and Slavery," which included full discussion of events in the United States. This journal, the *Historisch-politische Blätter für das katholische Deutschland*, had earlier provided extensive coverage of the War between the States, most of it blasting the North for hypocrisy (since northerners condemned slavery while they profited from the slave trade and the economic fruits of slavery). The journal also defended the Catholic Church as a perennial guardian of the humanity of Africans while attacking Protestants for their inability to agree on what Scripture taught about slavery. Münz recapitulated these criticisms while also asserting unequivocally "the incompatibility of slavery with the basic conception of Christianity." He closed his report with a chilling prophecy: "The North can free the slaves with force, but it cannot civilize them and deliver them from contempt and mistreatment. Here no one can help except the Church, whose main task is precisely this concern."[3] In 1868, when this article was written, what would prove to be the long history of American contempt and mistreatment of former slaves was barely under way. In fact, it continued until "the church" did do something about it, although it was not the Roman Catholic Church that led the way.

In November 1900 the nation returned President William McKinley to office for a second term in a comfortable Republican victory over his Democratic challenger, William Jennings Bryan. During the campaign, Bryan had distributed a pamphlet by the Negro National Democratic League that attacked U.S. oppression of the Filipino people in the name of those who knew firsthand what it meant to suffer from official American subjugation.[4] Bryan's support for black causes could not be too aggressive, however, since he needed the electoral votes of the Democratic Solid South, where the process of black disenfranchisement begun shortly after the Civil War was now nearly complete. In that presidential election, voter turnout (as a percentage of a state's population) ranged as high as 41% in Colorado, while the ratio in most northern and western states averaged between 20% and 33%. (In this period before female suffrage, these figures represented a reasonably high turnout.) But in most of the states of the former Confederacy, with their large black populations, it was another story. African Americans were almost entirely excluded from the polls, and whites had little incentive to vote in the general election, where the outcome was foreordained in favor of Democratic candidates. Thus, the turnout in these states was abysmally low—10% or less of state population in Arkansas, Alabama, and Florida; 5% or less in Georgia, Louisiana, Mississippi, and South Carolina.[5]

In the immediate wake of the election, the Rev. Francis Grimké presented a notable series of lectures to the Fifteenth Street Presbyterian Church in Washington, D.C., over which he had presided for more than twenty years. Grimké was a former slave who had studied at Lincoln University, Howard University, and Princeton Theological Seminary before beginning his long pastorate in Washington. On November 20, 1900, he lectured on the subject "Discouragements: Hostility of the Press, Silence and Cowardice of the Pulpit." The address singled out the South for special rebuke but also spoke implicitly of the whole nation:

> Lawlessness is increasing in the South. After thirty-three years of freedom, our civil and political rights are still denied us; the Fourteenth and Fifteenth Amendments to the Constitution are still a dead letter. . . . The determination to keep us in a state of civil and political inferiority and to surround us with such conditions as will tend to crush out of us a manly and self-respecting spirit is stronger now than it was at the close of the war. The fixed purpose and determination of the Southern whites is to negative these great amendments, to eliminate entirely the Negro as a political factor. . . . If he dares to think otherwise, or aspires to cast a ballot, or to become anything more than a servant, he is regarded as an impudent and dangerous Negro, and according to the most recent declaration of that old slave-holding and lawless spirit, all such Negroes are to be driven out of the South, or compelled by force, by what is known as the shot-gun policy, to renounce their rights as men and as American citizens.[6]

A week later Grimké continued his series by lecturing on "The General Government" and "Political Parties" as "Sources from Which No Help May Be Expected." Here the national focus of his indictment was explicit: "The white people in the South, and the white people in the North, as well, who sympathize with the Southern estimate of the

Negro, had just as well understand, once for all, that the Negro is a man and an American citizen, and that he will never be satisfied until he is treated as man, and as a full-fledged citizen."[7]

A full lifetime after Grimké's lectures, on February 18, 1965, Jimmy Lee Jackson took part in a nighttime voter-registration march in Marion, Alabama. The march was designed to proceed from the Mount Zion Baptist Church to the Perry County jail, which was located only a block from the church. Jackson at twenty-six was the youngest deacon at Marion's Saint James Baptist Church; already he had tried to register to vote on five separate occasions, but to no avail. Earlier in the week the *Times-Journal* in nearby Selma had published an advertisement sponsored by the local Citizens Council that linked the Voting Rights Act of 1964 to an earlier plan for racial equality published by the American Communist Party. The February 18 march was led by the Rev. James Dobynes. It was stopped at some distance from the jail by a large contingent of Alabama state troopers. When Rev. Dobynes knelt on the street to pray before returning to the church, he was assaulted by troopers and then dragged by his feet toward the jail. The remaining policemen waded into the column of marchers and sent participants scattering in all directions. Jimmy Lee Jackson, along with his mother and his grandfather, eighty-two-year-old Cager Lee, took refuge in a nearby café. Troopers pursued them into the café, where they beat Jackson's mother to the floor and also struck his grandfather. When Jackson tried to shield his mother, he was shot twice in the stomach and then hustled by troops out the door, where he collapsed. Jackson was taken to a hospital in Selma, where on Tuesday, February 23, the head of the Alabama state police personally served him with an arrest warrant.[8]

Jackson died on February 26. That night at Brown Chapel in Selma, James Bevel of the Southern Christian Leadership Conference preached a memorial sermon to a mass meeting. His texts were Acts 12:2–3 ("He [Herod] killed James the brother of John with the sword; and when he saw that it pleased the Jews, he proceeded to arrest Peter also") and Esther 4:8 ("Mordecai also gave him [the king's servant] a copy of the written decree issued in Susa for their [the Jews'] destruction, that he might show it to Esther and explain it to her and charge her to go to the king to make supplication to him and entreat for her people"). These passages allowed Bevel to identify the biblical kings, Herod and Mordecai's Ahasuerus, with Alabama's governor, George Wallace.

In 1965 the Fourteenth Amendment had been the law of the land for nearly a century. It defined American citizenship as belonging to "all persons born or naturalized in the United States," and it stipulated that no state could "deprive any person of life, liberty, or property, without due process of law; nor deny to any person within its jurisdiction the equal protection of the laws." In 1956 there were in Alabama about 500,000 unregistered African Americans of voting age. In the presidential election of 1964, when Lyndon Johnson's name was kept off the ballot in Alabama because of his support for the 1964 Civil Rights Act, the state's total vote was just short of 690,000 (that vote was divided 69.5% for Barry Goldwater and 30.5% for an unpledged slate of Democratic electors).

In the wake of the civil rights movement in which Jimmy Lee Jackson was murdered, African Americans finally won their own enfranchisement and began significantly expanded contributions at all levels of electoral politics. But racially defined voting remained almost as strong as in the day of

Sgt. Simmons, the Rev. Grimké, and Jimmy Lee Jackson. In 2000 white evangelical Protestants supported George Bush over Al Gore by 68% to 30%. In 2004 the white evangelical vote went to Bush over John Kerry by 78% to 21%. In 2000 Al Gore won 91% of the black Protestant vote; in 2004 John Kerry captured 86%.[9] Early in 2004, polling by Stanley Greenberg divided the core constituencies of the Republican and Democratic parties by variables featuring race, religion, wealth, region, gender, and age. Of all groups differentiated by these variables, the largest advantage in party identification was found among blacks, who favored the Democrats by 78 percentage points. The next largest was among white evangelical and fundamentalist Protestants, who favored the Republicans by 49 percentage points.[10] In light of these dramatic partisan differences keyed to race and religion, it is pertinent to remember one more fact documented by a wealth of polling—that the two identifiable groups within the American populace standing closest to each other on questions of religious belief and moral practice are white evangelicals and black Protestants.

These snapshots from 1863, 1868, 1900, 1965, and the early twenty-first century outline the terrain covered in this short history. It is a terrain defined by the intersection of politics, religion, and race. By race, I am referring primarily to the dynamic relationship between whites and blacks, though fuller attention to this subject would also show how religious factors have affected the American political history of southern Europeans, Jews, the Irish, Hispanics, and Asians as well.

For three out of the four great transformations in American history, potent combinations of race and religion were the engines that drove political change. Those transformative periods were the antebellum years from 1830 to 1860, when slavery came to overwhelm all other issues on the political landscape; the postbellum years from 1865 to roughly 1900, when the nation gave up on the project of equal rights for all and left African Americans unprotected in the civil sphere; and the recent past from the 1950s into the early twenty-first century, when the battle for civil rights was finally won, but with unanticipated spin-off effects and ironic consequences. The one exception to the rule that race in league with religion drove American political transformations was the 1930s, when economic pressures arising from the Great Depression changed American politics in ways only marginally affected by race and religion.

This short history offers an interpretation of the other three transformations in which I try to show how the concerns of race have combined with the interests of religion to decisively shape the course of American politics. It also tries to show that, although race and religion combined differently in each of the three transformations, the successive combinations have constituted a single, continuous narrative from the slave revolt of Nat Turner in 1830 to the reelection of George W. Bush in 2004. Defining the political transformations and trying to explain how race and religion dictated the shape of their development are the major concerns of this book.

Naturally, I am aware that many of the issues and incidents canvassed here fairly cry out for moral evaluation. For the most part, however, I have tried harder to describe than to judge. Especially in our era that has become so alert to discrimination of all sorts, it may be more valuable to show how a continuous history developed than to provide a continual evaluation of that history. Yet because the ties among race, religion, and politics have been so intimate in American history—and because these ties have produced such momentous consequences—I do pause at the end of the historical exposition to attempt a broader religious interpretation. That interpretation makes use of Calvinist theology, a strand of moral reasoning that has been well represented in both black and white American churches, and in secularized forms more broadly in the society. As I bring my history to a close in this way, I am fully aware of the irony that what I present as a response to the great racial-religious-political entanglements of American history has been itself one of the chief contributors to the moral predicaments created by those entanglements.

⁓

This book is based on my own research on the Civil War period and on twentieth-century white American evangelicals, combined with appreciative reading of the splendid scholarship that now exists for the years of Reconstruction and the modern civil rights era. While I was finishing an earlier study that dealt at length with the intensive debates over the Bible and slavery that galvanized much of American society before the Civil War, I was asked to propose a lecture series at Princeton University.[11] At the time I was also reading David Chappell's *Stone of Hope*, with its forceful arguments about the key place of African-American religion and white southern Protestantism in the civil rights movement.[12] In addition, I was being exposed to provocative work by Dennis Dickerson and Thabiti Anyabwile that charted the relatively neglected history of African-American religious thought,[13] and I was reading an outstanding new textbook on the Civil War and Reconstruction.[14] Moreover, this reading and writing was taking place in Washington, D.C., at the Library of Congress during the academic year

2004–05, when all Washington was abuzz about the "values voting" of white evangelicals that carried George W. Bush to victory in that November's presidential election.

When these disparate trajectories began to intersect in my mind, it seemed immediately obvious that they made up not only an interesting series of parallel case studies, but a single connected history. The lectures at Princeton in the fall of 2006 and this "short history," which expands on those lectures, try to justify that initial impression. During my work on this book, the intensively researched three volumes of Taylor Branch's history of "America in the King Years" headed an ever-growing list of outstanding titles on relevant subjects from which I harvested much information and many insights.[15] Authors of these studies, many of which are acknowledged in the notes, have labored diligently to rescue the history of the Civil War era, postbellum American history, and the civil rights movement from romantic mythmaking on the one side and cynical debunking on the other. None of the scholars on whom I relied is responsible for how I have used his or her work in forming my own judgments about the general importance of race in American political history, or about the critical role that religion has played in making race so salient in politics. Yet the cumulative result of their insights, added to the findings of my own research, drive the conviction developed in this short history—that race and religion have acted together powerfully not only to shape the nation's political history, but also to define the nation's central moral problem.

CHAPTER I

The Bible, Slavery, and the "Irrepressible Conflict"

Events from antebellum America have decisively shaped all subsequent American history in large part because of pervasive interconnections among religion, politics, slavery, and race. Those interconnections explain why it is so easy, when reading the fervent sermons of the early civil rights movement from the 1950s and 1960s, to imagine that they are reprising the fervent sermons of the 1850s and 1860s.[1] They explain why the dynamics of regional politics today so faithfully replicate the political geography of the mid-nineteenth century. And they explain why current debates over the size and exercise of national government authority so often arise from circumstances related to race or religion.

Connections between then and now remain strong. The religious baptism of racially based political positions, which occurred with increasing force from 1830, permanently stratified American political allegiance such that patterns from that earlier period have continued through a host of momentous alterations to define the present. Moreover, the style of religion that became important in the antebellum period—for whites and blacks, for religious practitioners and the indifferent—grew out of the strong early American presence of broadly Calvinistic faiths, and the public strategies of that religious type (more than their specific religious content) have also remained important.

From its earliest days, the political history of the United States was driven by debates over slavery, debates that became more intensely religious as the sectional crisis moved toward war. The key matter for what came later was that antebellum religious controversy over slavery overwhelmed and confused religious consideration of race. In turn, the confusion between slavery and race explains why the Civil War, which so decisively answered many other national questions, left the question of race open as a festering problem for future generations. The Civil War—as a conflict to define the Union, determine the legitimacy of slavery, and specify the limits of states rights—was also fundamentally a religious battle over how to interpret the Bible and how to promote moral norms in public life. The shape of political, racial, and religious strife that led to the war established patterns that, despite many significant changes in later generations, remain in place to the present day.

American Political Stratification, 1830 to the Present

The general importance of the race-religion connection in American history is suggested by two matters: the results of elections and the perpetual conflict over whether and how to use national power to shape social and cultural norms. It is of course true that other forces—involving especially wealth and warfare—have also greatly influenced elections

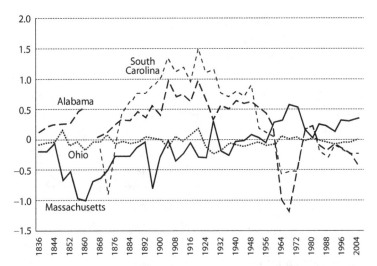

Figure 1.1. State Democratic Vote as Percentage of National Democratic Vote, 1836–2004

and decisively shaped the use of national power, but race in connection with religion has always figured prominently in both.

Presidential elections, as charted in figure 1.1, provide a bird's-eye view of the long-term picture for electoral results.[2] The figure displays results of presidential balloting for Alabama and South Carolina (which stand for the eleven states of the former Confederacy), Massachusetts (which generally tracks New England), and Ohio (which is representative for much of the Midwest). Voting results from these four states provide a rough outline of the nation's political history. The central fact shown by the figure is that where lines are tangled and where they reveal clear differentiation both reflect a history fundamentally keyed to race and religion. Thus, there is a tangle of regional political allegiances for the period 1836 to 1864, followed by a long period of regional differentiation from 1876 through 1948, followed by another period of tangled regional allegiance from 1952 to 1984, followed by another period of regional differentiation from 1988 through the present, though in this last period of differentiation the separation is not as stark as for the earlier period from Reconstruction through World War II. In all instances, race and religion provide much of the explanation for the stability and the changes.

To explain the figure in a little more detail, it standardizes the results of presidential voting for each state relative to the nation at each four-year national election from 1836 through 2004.[3] The proportions record a state's popular vote for that year's Democratic candidate divided by that year's national vote.[4] Thus, in 1836 the Democratic candidate, Martin Van Buren, won 55.3% of the vote in Alabama and 50.8% of the national popular vote; the figure thus records a proportion of 1.09 (55.3% divided by 50.8%). For Massachusetts in 1860, the Democratic candidate Stephen A. Douglas won 20.2% of the popular vote and the southern Democratic candidate John C. Breckinridge won 3.6%, for a total Democratic vote of 23.8%; nationally these two factions of the Democratic Party totaled 47.6% of the popular vote; the figure thus records a proportion of 0.50 for Massachusetts (20.2% plus 3.6% divided by 47.6%). For 2000 the national percentage for Democratic candidate Al Gore was 48.4% and in South Carolina 40.9%; the South Carolina proportion is recorded as 0.85 (40.9% divided by 48.4%). By recording proportions instead of raw votes, it is easier to visualize long-term trends and to even out close elections with the occasional landslides that tend to obscure long-term relations of state vote to national totals.[5]

The political history summarized by the figure passed through several distinct stages. From 1836 to 1852, Jacksonian

Democrats and the opponents of Jackson who united to form the Whig Party remained more or less competitive in all areas of the country. For example, in 1848, when the Whig Zachary Taylor defeated the Democrat Lewis Cass and the Free Soil candidate Martin Van Buren, the northern states Maine, New Hampshire, Michigan, and Wisconsin voted for the Democrat while the southern states Florida, Georgia, Louisiana, North Carolina, Tennessee, Kentucky, and Maryland voted for the Whig.

After the political effects of slave controversy as backed by religion had hardened, however, it was another story. Regions of the country became much more firmly fixed in their electoral allegiances. Although this fixing can be accounted for by a wide range of factors besides race and religion, race and religion were nonetheless of first importance. A comparison of the states that had made up the Confederacy with the states of New England and the states of the eastern Midwest (Illinois, Indiana, Michigan, Ohio, Wisconsin) illustrates the hardening of those regional markers (see table 1.1). In New England and the eastern Midwest from 1880 through 1916, the Republican candidate won 91 out of 110 state contests for president (83%). From 1920 through 1984, in the 187 state presidential contests in these two regions, and despite the great popularity of Franklin Delano Roosevelt in his four races, the Republican candidate won 125 out of 187 times (67%). Beginning with the Bush-Dukakis election in 1988, however, a strong reversal occurred, with the Democratic candidate victorious in 40 of 55 state races in the two regions since that year (73%).

It is a different picture entirely for the states of the former Confederacy. From 1880 through 1916, the Democratic candidate won every presidential race in every one of these eleven states (110 out of 110). From 1920 through 1948

TABLE 1.1

Democratic Victories in Presidential Elections, 1880–2004
(by state)

Years	Confederate South[a]	New England[b]	Eastern Midwest[c]
1880–1916	110/110 (100%)	10/60 (17%)	9/50 (18%)
1920–1948	82/88 (93%)	17/48 (35%)	18/40 (45%)
1952–1976	43[d]/77 (56%)	17/42 (40%)	10/35 (29%)
1980–2004	9/77 (12%)	26/42 (62%)	15/35 (43%)

[a] Alabama, Arkansas, Florida, Georgia, Louisiana, Mississippi, North Carolina, South Carolina, Tennessee, Texas, Virginia.

[b] Connecticut, Maine, Massachusetts, New Hampshire, Rhode Island, Vermont.

[c] Illinois, Indiana, Michigan, Ohio, Wisconsin.

[d] Includes five state victories for George Wallace's American Party in 1968 and one state victory for an unpledged set of electors in 1960.

Source: *Presidential Elections, 1789–2000* (Washington, D.C.: CQ Press, 2002).

(and counting the States' Rights victories of Strom Thurmond in 1948 as Democratic victories), the Democratic candidate lost only 6 times out of 88 state contests—and 5 of those were in 1928 when voters in the strongly evangelical states of Florida, North Carolina, Tennessee, Texas, and Virginia chose Herbert Hoover over the Roman Catholic Al Smith. From 1952 through 1976, and despite the strong national popularity of Dwight D. Eisenhower, Democratic candidates still won almost half the state contests (37 of 77, 48%). Beginning with the first campaign of Ronald Reagan in 1980 through the second campaign of George W. Bush in 2004, an even stronger reversal occurred than in New England and the eastern Midwest; Democratic candidates won only 9 out of 77 state contests (12%) in this former bulwark of Democratic support.

To indicate the importance of these regional hegemonies, it is useful to note that since the 1830s the combined electoral votes of the eleven former Confederate states have represented about one-fourth of the national total (ranging from 94 to 127 total votes and from 23.4% to 26.7% of the whole). Moreover, it is also pertinent that in those states, with their strong African-American populations, most blacks were excluded from the polls until the 1960s. Additionally, white evangelical Protestants have been strongly overrepresented in these states as compared to the rest of the country.

Given electoral realities as represented by these strong political bifurcations, it means that the ideologies that undergirded politics, particularly in functionally one-party regions of the country, and particularly in the Solid South, must be considered significant for the nation's political history as a whole. And if those ideologies were strongly shaped by ideas about race that were supported by religious convictions, then race and religion must be considered determinative influences on national politics.

The political influence of race and religion went deeper, however, than just the result of elections. The race-political connection has always been a national reality and not just a parochial relationship limited to the South. Northern economic interests participated fully in the slave system itself.[6] Throughout American history, integration of freed blacks into northern communities always proceeded with painful timidity.[7] Even before African-American populations rose significantly outside the South, racial exclusion was a long-standing feature of many communities, especially in the Midwest.[8] (See table 1.2 for the national distribution of African-American population.) As indicated by an ongoing succession of crises—the Chicago race riot of 1919; the racial strife embroiling Catholic parishes after World War II; the

TABLE 1.2
National Distribution of African-American Population
(percentage)

	1860	1920	1980
Confederate South[a]	81.6	77.1	45.3
New England[b]	0.6	0.8	1.8
Mid Atlantic[c]	2.9	5.7	16.5
Union South[d]	13.1	8.5	8.8
East Midwest[e]	1.4	4.9	17.2
West Midwest[f]	0.1	2.3	1.9
Mountain[g]	0.1	0.3	1.1
Pacific[h]	0.1	0.5	7.5
Total	6,580,000	12,861,000	34,660,000

[a] Alabama, Arkansas, Florida, Georgia, Louisiana, Mississippi, North Carolina, South Carolina, Tennessee, Texas, Virginia.

[b] Connecticut, Maine, Massachusetts, New Hampshire, Rhode Island, Vermont.

[c] New Jersey, New York, Pennsylvania.

[d] Delaware, Kentucky, Maryland, Missouri, West Virginia. (Slave states that did not join the Confederacy.)

[e] Illinois, Indiana, Michigan, Ohio, Wisconsin.

[f] Iowa, Kansas, Minnesota, Nebraska, North Dakota, Oklahoma, South Dakota.

[g] Alaska, Arizona, Colorado, Idaho, Montana, Nebraska, New Mexico, Utah, Wyoming.

[h] California, Hawaii, Oregon, Washington.

Source: Susan B. Carter et al., eds., *Historical Statistics of the United States: Millennial Edition* (New York: Cambridge University Press, 2006).

civil rights battles and riots of the 1960s in Chicago, Detroit, and Watts; the Rodney King beating in Los Angeles in 1991—racial antagonism has been a permanent feature in the North throughout the twentieth century and beyond. Political fixations dominated by race have obviously been central to elections in the former Confederate South and the slave states that remained in the Union. If they have been less obviously central in the nonslave states, it has been due at least in part to the fact that northerners were reluctant to acknowledge how deeply they had been involved in the system of slavery and how widely they shared in dismissive attitudes toward African Americans.

The broader, implicit issue that has always been connected in American history with explicit matters of race and religion is the question of federal power. Intense differences of opinion about this grand issue were critical during the confederation and constitutional years that immediately followed the War for Independence, and they have been critical ever since. Actual implementation of ideals for central government—whether it is considered a necessary evil to be constrained or a potential good to be used cautiously for common betterment—has always been extremely complicated, with deeds never lining up squarely with professed convictions. Nonetheless, a clear conceptual divide was present from the start.

On the one side has been a classically republican ideology that led to the views of Thomas Jefferson about the intuitive merits of independent yeomen farmers and then to the convictions of Andrew Jackson about "the common man." This ideology dominated the Democratic Party until the early twentieth century, was a central conviction of the Dixie Democrats into the 1960s, and has been prominent in the Republican Party since the 1870s. From this perspective, big government is bad government. Central government actions are to be curtailed at all costs in order to let local authorities and local institutions control local circumstances. In this perspective, individuals, families, and self-selected interest groups flourish best when national government protects them from outside forces, not least the force of central government itself.

The opposite opinion was represented by what can be called a liberal republican ideology. It took shape in Alexander Hamilton's vision of an economically empowering central government and then in the Whig Party's addition of morality to the earlier confidence of the Federalists in the use of central government authority.[9] This ideology strongly shaped the Whigs and then the Republicans at least through the climactic election of 1876; early in the twentieth century it was strong among Progressive Democrats and Republicans, and then with New Deal Democrats; since World War II it has been widely prevalent among Democrats, but also among some Republicans on some issues. From this perspective, somewhat bigger government can be better government. The right kind of central government actions are encouraged in order to assist local authorities and local institutions in making local circumstances better. In this perspective, individuals, families, and self-selected interest groups flourish best when national government aids them in dealing with the broader world.

Of course, in American history clear ideological divisions have always been complicated by practice. Andrew Jackson, as an important instance, remained true to antigovernment type when he opposed the Bank of the United States and expanded the franchise to include virtually all white males. Yet Jackson never set great store by consistency. He used the weight of central government to expel the Cherokee from Georgia, even though these native Americans had embraced republican politics and the Christian faith for themselves. Jackson also agreed to a high national tariff, and he was willing to threaten states that presumed to nullify the tariff in their own jurisdictions. His foundational antigovernment convictions, in other words, did not automatically predict his political actions.

The Mexican War of 1846–1848 also obscured ideological clarity. Democrats were willing to use national military force, but for the purpose of expanding the territory of the United States in which the federal government would not otherwise interfere. Many Whigs opposed the exercise of national military power in the Mexican War in order to limit the expansion of the southern United States, where federal authority was not welcome.

The key matter to be stressed is that, from the 1770s to the 1910s, virtually all debates about the exercise of national political power in American political history were arguments in which either slavery or race was central.[10] In the century since 1910, many of these debates have again featured race. From the angry response of the American patriots to Governor Dunmore's executive order in 1775 that offered freedom to Virginia slaves who came over to the British, through negotiations concerning the Three-Fifths Clause in the Constitution that resulted in increased congressional representation and electoral clout for the slaveholding states, questions of race and the location of supreme political authority were central in the era of national founding. They remained central in later controversies over the admission of new states, national taxing policies, the Civil War itself, Reconstruction, Populist and Progressive reforms at the turn of the twentieth century—and then in debates over civil rights after World War II and the size of federal budgets in the Bush, Clinton, and Bush administrations. What David Brion Davis once wrote about South Carolina's effort to nullify the tariff approved by President Jackson could, *mutatis mutandis*, be applied to many other times and places in American history: "by forcing a redefinition of state sovereignty and of the limits of national power," South Carolina found "the tariff issue . . . an ideal testing ground for the defense of slavery without risking the explosive effects of debating the morality of slaveholding."[11] American controversy over the exercise of central government authority has almost always been either dominated by race or in some meaningful way affected by race.

Polarization over the exercise of federal government power may thus be as meaningful a gauge of the influence of race in American political history as direct debates over slavery or civil rights. The fiction has been easy to sustain that slavery and civil rights were regional questions, important mostly or even only for the South. Refocusing historical analysis to controversies about central government authority makes it easier to grasp the national influence of race in American political history.

In sum, the bearing of race on American politics is visible both directly in electoral history and indirectly for issues concerning the exercise of central government authority. For both matters, to think of American politics and not also to think about race is to miss what actually went on. The rest of this book takes the race-political connection as a premise; its main burden is to indicate how religion interacted with race in shaping the nation's political course.

Calvinism as a Template for Religious Engagement with Public Life

In the history of the United States, religion has often functioned publicly in Calvinist form. From the earliest Puritan settlements of the seventeenth century, a style of direct and activistic application of religious principles to public problems has defined a norm for those like the Puritans, who professed a Protestant Calvinist faith, but also for many whose religions have been far removed from Calvinism. This way of describing connections between religion and public life was drawn with special force by André Siegfried, a French visitor to North America in the 1920s who recorded impressions about the United States that were almost as prescient as those offered by his countryman, Alexis de Tocqueville, nearly a century earlier. Siegfried, like de Tocqueville, found religion a key to American politics. And to explain what he viewed as an especially prominent American trait, he turned to religious history. In his view, the "religious mysticism and political cynicism" that he considered characteristic of the Lutheran lands of continental Europe could not be more different from what he discovered in the United States. Here, rather, Siegfried saw Protestants of Calvinistic inclinations at work, by which he meant not something narrowly denominational but the activistic ethos bequeathed by the broadly Puritan-evangelical-Methodist-voluntary pattern that became so dominant in nineteenth-century American culture. So defined, Siegfried held that "the Calvinist" felt himself burdened with "a mission to carry out; namely to purify the life of the community and to uplift the state. He cannot admit two separate spheres of action, for he believes that the influence of Christ should dominate every aspect of life."[12]

Siegfried's observation extended what a modern historian, W. Fred Graham, once wrote about the contrast between Martin Luther and John Calvin: "Calvin was more concerned than Luther to tell soldiers how they must fight . . . and also more concerned to tell the Geneva city Council how it should govern. Luther turned over such legal questions to the political arm, and this in no small measure helped produce in Germany and Scandinavia a more peaceful, less revolutionary movement, when compared with the government-toppling cadres issuing from Geneva."[13] Such contrasts could be extended by comparing a broadly Calvinist approach to public life with an Anabaptist approach, for the Anabaptists were always much more intentionally suspicious of public activism than the Calvinists. Or the contrast could be made with Roman Catholicism, which looked to formal church-state establishments to accomplish society-wide goals rather than to energetic lay mobilization; similarly, Catholicism could encourage a spiritual embrace of unjust suffering instead of a direct challenge to righting the injustice causing the suffering, which would be the ordinary Calvinist procedure.[14] An additional contrast could be found between Calvinism and secular libertarianism, where other people's problems are simply other people's problems unless they inhibit the exercise of personal freedom.

For André Siegfried, the reason for focusing on the Calvinist legacy was to explain the American political sphere more generally. Because of how important the energetic voluntarism of a broad Calvinist trajectory had proven, it colored all of American public life. In fact, he thought the Puritan-evangelical heritage held the secret for explaining the American political style that so often baffled Europeans: "Every American is at heart an evangelist, be he a [Woodrow] Wilson, a [William Jennings] Bryan, or a [John D.] Rockefeller. He cannot leave people alone, and he constantly feels the urge to preach."[15]

This political style has often been expressed in American history through employment of the Bible for the purpose of public moral persuasion. The pro and con debates over whether the Scriptures sanctioned slavery provided the most spectacular instance of this phenomenon, but use of a scriptural word has also featured large in debates over Indian removal, temperance reform, and—most significantly—civil rights. In these and many other cases, the broadly Calvinist approach has taken shape in a direct biblical effort to influence political decisions. The result has been to give public argument a particular intensity—both when it takes place as Scripture battling against Scripture and when it occurs as Scripture battling against those who vehemently dispute the relevance of Scripture. In both cases, intense moral focus allows for a broad appeal to the public but also broad-based political antagonism, or culture wars.

This mode of religiously charged, public moral argument received its definitive expression in the decades before the Civil War. Yet it continues to exert considerable influence in American public life—however modified or diffused—in direct line with its extraordinary influence in that earlier period and through the continuing actions of citizens who bring their religious values into the public sphere directly, forthrightly, and with passion.

Religious Factors in the Divide over Slavery

The emergence of religiously charged debate over slavery resulted from three miscalculations by the Founders. First was the hope that compromises in the Constitution would eliminate later controversy over slavery. The compromise involved, first, specifying a date after which the salve trade could be legislated (1808), which favored those nervous about legitimating chattel bondage in a republic that had so recently trumpeted its liberation from the "enslavement" of the British Parliament (art. 1, sec. 9); but also, second, an agreement to let slaves count as three-fifths of a person, which made the states with many slaves both more powerful and less democratic than the states with few or none (art. 1, sec. 2).

The second miscalculation was to think that removing the national government from the religion business would make religion a noncontroversial factor in national political life. To be sure, when in 1791 the First Amendment to the Constitution announced its truce over such matters— "Congress shall make no law respecting an establishment of religion, or prohibiting the free exercise thereof"—five of the nation's fourteen states provided tax support for Christian ministers, and those five plus seven others continued religious tests for public office.[16] Only Virginia and Rhode Island practiced a separation of church and state where government provided no money for churches and posed no religious conditions for participation in public life. As Roman Catholics, Jews, and members of other non-Protestant faiths would long experience, the American separation of church and state did not guarantee complete religious freedom. Nonetheless, the amendment was meant to defuse the intense, often violent conflicts that in Europe had been commonplace because of the role given to state-established churches in setting public policy, distributing public funds, and controlling public education. In avoiding many European problems, the Founders succeeded. But they did not reckon on the new form of religion that would prevail in the new United States.

Thus, the third miscalculation concerned the character of religion in the new nation. Moderate and conservative Founders hoped for the continual influence of the churches that had been either established in the colonies (Congregationalists in New England, Episcopalians in the southern colonies) or quasi-established (Presbyterians in the middle colonies). They expected these churches to act as sources of order, decorum, and social control. By contrast, progressive Founders, like Thomas Jefferson, hoped for the spread of Enlightenment faiths that more closely resembled deism than traditional Christianity. Jefferson's egregiously inaccurate prediction, made in 1822, was that "the present generation will see Unitarianism become the general religion of the United States."[17] Yet already by that date it was obvious that both of these expectations were faulty.

Instead, religion in America was coming to be dominated by evangelical sects that featured supernatural faith, precritical reading of the Bible, and an aggressive exploitation of the democratic deeds and rhetoric of the American Revolution. In these sects, intense concern for personal transformation was balanced by a desire to exert informal influence in society. The leading churches from the colonial era, Episcopalians and Congregationalists, adjusted slowly to the new freedoms of the early republic and so fell behind. Methodists, Baptists, Disciples, "Christians"—even fledgling African-American churches—which embraced those freedoms with determination, flourished.[18] From the American Revolution to the Civil War, the rate of religious adherence advanced almost twice as fast as the rate of growth of the nation's rapidly expanding population, and it did so because the aggressively populist denominations were so successful. In 1790 there existed less than a thousand Methodist churches; by 1860 there were almost twenty thousand. In the same period, Baptists grew from under a thousand churches to more than twelve thousand; Disciples/Christians leapt from zero to over two thousand; and Presbyterians, who adjusted more rapidly to new conditions than the Congregationalists and Episcopalians, from about seven hundred to about sixty-four hundred. The census of 1860 found that more than 95% of the places of worship enumerated for the whole country were Protestant, and over 88% of those worship sites were Protestant of British origin, with the vast majority belonging to the more actively populist denominations. The ways of addressing the public pursued by these energetic Protestants set the tone and established the possibilities for many adherents of other religions—and also eventually for significant numbers of those who abandoned religion.

The crucial matter was aggressive self-organization combined with democratic convictions. This energizing burst of American Protestantism was driven by *voluntary* means. Yet through these voluntary means the churches shaped the entire national culture.

The reality of what actually happened, rather than the mistaken expectations of the Founders, eventually led to the emergence of slavery as an explosive political issue thoroughly bound up with religious concerns. Constitutional compromise did not eliminate slavery as a source of political controversy. The First Amendment increased rather than decreased the public influence of organized religion. And the religion that came to prevail featured not elites guiding the masses, but lay empowerment, lay reliance on Scripture, and lay voluntary initiative.

For the charged politics that led to civil war, the struggle in 1819–20 over the admission of Missouri to the Union has recently been described as a "turning point" where "the maturation of proslavery thought" came to public expression in such a way as to begin "the prolonged crisis of the Union."[19] Especially since the Missouri Compromise that resolved this controversy was followed shortly thereafter by the Denmark Vesey slave rebellion in South Carolina—and a national upsurge in attention to slavery in generally—it is plausible to view the early 1820s as the pivot pointing toward sectional conflict.

But when religion is added to the picture, it is even more plausible to view the years immediately surrounding (1830) as the moment when the festering agitation over slavery, which had been threatening to break loose from before the national founding, finally burst onto center stage in American public life. That explosion occurred in no small measure because this was the point when religion entered fully into the debate. The conjunction of events was striking. In 1829 the free black David Walker published the era's most incendiary attack on slavery by an African American—perhaps by anyone. Uncompromising application of the Christian Scriptures was a major feature of Walker's dramatic tract, *Appeal ... to the Coloured Citizens of the World*: "Can the American preacher appeal unto God, the Maker and Searcher of hearts, and tell him, with the Bible in their hands, that they made no distinction on account of men's colour?"[20] If Walker's message was shrugged aside in Boston, where it was published, it was not as easy to shrug aside the rebellion led by Nat Turner in Southampton County, Virginia, two years later. Turner's own confession, which was taken down before his execution, used the language of Christian apocalypse and stressed the visions he had received of biblical scenes. If few Americans allowed that such visions were grounds for rebellion, the depth of Turner's apocalypticism did reveal how thoroughly at least some part of the nation's slave population had internalized at least some Christian elements in their own understanding of human bondage.[21]

In response to Nat Turner's rebellion, legislatures cracked down on slaves in many southern states and restricted rights of free blacks in some northern states. In reaction to this response, antislave reformers greatly increased their efforts to contest what they called "sin" or a "malum in se."[22] They were spurred on in these efforts by heightened awareness of the steady march toward emancipation in the British Empire. The year 1831 witnessed the first issue of William Lloyd Garrison's *The Liberator*, which proclaimed antislavery a higher law than even the Scriptures. But it was also the year of Charles G. Finney's revivalistic conquest of Rochester, New York, and the emergence of Finney as the North's most visible promoter of evangelical Christianity, which by then had become the nation's dominant expression of religion. Parliament's final action to suppress slavery in the British Empire followed in 1833. A year later, Finney published in New York City a widely read series of lectures, *Revivals of Religion*, which he offered for sale in order to rescue his publisher from a financial embarrassment caused by his strong abolitionist stand. In these lectures, Finney, as was his wont, left no doubt about his opinions:

> slavery is, pre-eminently, the *sin of the church*. . . . Let Christians of all denominations meekly but firmly come forth, and pronounce their verdict, let them clear their communions, and wash their hands of this thing, let them give forth and write on the head and front of his great abomination, SIN! and in three years, a public sentiment would be formed that would carry all before it, and there would not be a shackled slave, nor a bristling, cruel slave-driver in this land.[23]

Predictably, such charges produced outrage in the slaveholding South, which was even then undergoing its own process of evangelical conversion, a process that began later than in the North but was advancing with even broader effect.[24] Thus it was that abolitionist appeals to Christian principles as support for emancipation produced detailed scriptural arguments from the South (and the North as well) to defend slavery as a divinely sanctioned institution. Biblical defenses of slavery were hardly a new thing; they had appeared intermittently in the United States from the 1770s in response to the attacks by British Quakers and Anglican evangelicals against the practice. But the use of Scripture to defend the American system of slavery became influential for the nation only when abolitionists after the time of Nat Turner began to mine the Bible for ammunition against the institution. As I have tried to show elsewhere, abolitionists who turned to Scripture for the attack on slavery were chagrined to find that the defenders of slavery could quote many more texts that simply took the institution for granted, or even regulated its operation, than there were passages that, even by implication, questioned its propriety.[25] Thus, when in 1837 Finney's acolyte Theodore Dwight Weld published *The Bible against Slavery*, abolitionists applauded Weld's passionate efforts to force the semantics of ancient Hebrew into an antislave posture. But proslavery advocates like Thornton Stringfellow of Virginia positively rejoiced because, as he demonstrated in 1841 with *A Brief Examination of Scripture Testimony on the Institution of Slavery* and then in numerous later adaptations of this work, it was relatively easy to show that Abraham, Moses, the Apostle Paul, and even Jesus himself either took the existence of slavery for granted or made no obvious moves to eliminate it.

Positioned in the middle between extremists like Weld and Stringfellow were many Bible-believing moderates who very much wanted to reject slavery but who also realized how important a reliance on the Bible had been for all of Protestant history—and especially for supporting the populist evangelical movements that had risen so powerfully in the new United States. Such ones found themselves in a dilemma. They wanted to go with Finney and Weld in attacking slavery, but they were held back by a sense that the antislave zeal of these crusaders was pushing them into dangerously loose distortions of Scripture. The Congregationalist Leonard Bacon, who was both strongly antislave and biblically conservative, concluded one careful analysis of the theological issue with these words: "the evidence that there were both slaves and masters of slaves in the churches founded and directed by the apostles, cannot be got rid of without resorting to *methods of interpretation which will get rid of everything.*" To Bacon, the well-intentioned and even Bible-quoting abolitionists who "torture the Scriptures into saying that which the anti-slavery theory requires them to say" did more harm to the Bible's authority than "the violence put upon the sacred records by High Churchmen, or by Universalists."[26]

From the early 1830s, when these positions on the Bible were staked out, until the early months of 1861, when the last round of published conflict took place between self-confident biblical antislavery and even more self-confident biblical proslavery, the question of slavery was debated just as earnestly for theological purposes as it was as a political problem. For the history of American politics, several important results flowed from these debates over what the Bible did or did not teach about slavery.

First, the debates were dividing the nation's evangelical churches against themselves during the years of U.S. history when these churches enjoyed an influence over public life greater than any other religious tradition has ever enjoyed at any other time. Beginning in the 1790s, mobilization by Methodists and Baptists, but also Presbyterians, Disciples, reforming Congregationalists, a host of sectarian groups, and even Episcopalians, had created the America that Alexis de Tocqueville discovered in the 1830s. Tocqueville noted that, unlike Europe, the American churches as formal institutions had little to do with the state, but also—again, unlike Europe—that a religious ethos exerted a pervasive pressure on American public life. Democratic, lay engagement with the Bible as a message of personal salvation, but also of social responsibility, had contributed greatly to the construction of American national culture.[27] Yet after de Tocqueville returned to France—from the 1830s onwards—the culture that had been built by lay religious agency was being torn apart by the antithetical conclusions on slavery that lay Bible interpreters discovered in the Scriptures.

Second, as C. C. Goen, Richard Carwardine, and other historians have demonstrated, what happened institutionally to the large national churches and the most widely spread religious voluntary societies exerted an unusual impact on the nation.[28] When John C. Calhoun in March 1850 addressed the U.S. Senate for almost the last time, the fact of ecclesiastical schism loomed large in his political analysis. After Calhoun described "the great religious denominations" as powerful cords of "a spiritual and ecclesiastical nature," he then asserted that these connections "contributed greatly to strengthen the bonds of the Union. The ties which had held each denomination together formed a strong cord to hold the whole Union together." Calhoun then went on to make a prediction that became justly famous: when all such bonds have snapped, "nothing will be left to hold the States together except force."[29]

Calhoun in 1850 was reflecting on a dismaying recent history of fragmenting national bonds.[30] In 1845 there had been about as many Methodist clergy as postal employees, who made up the largest nonmilitary department of the U.S. government. Were it not for the military buildup occasioned by the Mexican War, there would have been more active Methodist and Baptist ministers than U.S. military personnel. In 1845 the statistically "average" American in the course of a year probably heard more sermons from a Methodist minister than received pieces of mail. Along with Methodist churches, the churches of the Baptists and Presbyterians were distributed more widely in the nation than any single organization of any kind. The only national institutions that came close to the denominations were not publishers or, in this era before railroad expansion, businesses, but religious voluntary agencies like the American Bible Society. In 1845 the Methodist and Baptist churches could seat at one time well over half of the nation's population. Yet by the end of 1845, the national organizations of Methodists, Baptists, and Presbyterians, which had been built through the painstaking labor of thousands of self-sacrificing men and women, were divided. The Presbyterian schism of 1837 was prompted only in part by disagreements over slavery. The Methodist and Baptist divisions of 1844–45 were a direct result of disagreement over whether, respectively, a Methodist bishop and a Baptist missionary could own slaves. Calhoun in 1850 worried about the fate of the nation because he had seen what slavery had done to the national churches.

Only a short time before Calhoun made this speech, but in a more sanguine period of political and ecclesiastical history, a veteran Methodist Bishop, Nathan Bangs, had written about the inadvertent political effects of the unprecedented expansion of his denomination, which by then had reached into every corner of the land:

> Although it formed no part of the design of its [Methodism's] disciples to enter into the political speculations of the day, nor to intermeddle with the civil

affairs of the country, yet it is thought that its extensive spread in this country, the hallowing influence it has exerted in society in uniting in one compact body so many members, through the medium of an itinerant ministry, interchanging from north to south, and from east to west, has contributed not a little to the union and prosperity of the nation.[31]

When, in Bangs's terms, the unity and prosperity of the churches were threatened by division over slavery, so also was the unity and prosperity of the nation itself. If the churches, which were substantially responsible for constituting the national culture, could not resolve their differences, especially when they claimed to have the Word of God assisting them, what hope did the nation have?

A mere chronology cannot carry a full argument, but conjunctions of religious history and political history during the period 1830 to 1860 are still instructive. In 1832 and 1833, just as Britain finally decreed an end to slavery in the West Indies, South Carolina (the American state with closest ties to the West Indies) asserted its right to control its own destiny by nullifying a national tariff, and abolitionists, located overwhelmingly in the North, founded the American Anti-Slavery Society in imitation of the British example. In 1836 and 1837 Congress enacted a Gag Rule to table the accumulating pile of petitions from abolitionists; Elijah Lovejoy became the first abolitionist martyr when he was killed by a mob attacking his printing operation in Alton, Illinois; and the Presbyterian denomination divided into New School and Old School factions. In 1844 John C. Calhoun used his office as secretary of state under President Tyler to promote slave-state interests, and the Baptists and

Methodists divided over slavery. Shortly thereafter, the Wilmot Proviso prohibited slavery in states formed out of land taken from Mexico during the recent war. In the early 1850s Congress hammered out a compromise to deal with the new territories of Nebraska and Kansas, and Harriet Beecher Stowe's novel *Uncle Tom's Cabin*, with its overtly religious attack on slavery, was published to great acclaim in the North and great disdain in the South. In 1854 and 1855 George Fitzhugh brought out his *Sociology for the South*, which defended the slavery of all races by all races as superior to the social order of individualistic capitalism derived from John Locke, Adam Smith, and Thomas Jefferson; Know-Nothings won elections throughout the North with a strong anti-immigrant, anti-Catholic platform; and Kansas suffered bloody lawlessness as guerillas battled over whether to permit slavery in the new state. In 1857 the Supreme Court handed down its *Dred Scott* decision, which invalidated the Missouri Compromise of 1820 and denied that blacks, whether slave or free, could enjoy the rights of American citizens, while a new wave of revivals swept the urban North. These revivals were noteworthy for appealing to busy, sophisticated businessmen, but also for prohibiting discussion of controversial social issues like slavery.[32] In 1859 John Brown's raid on Harper's Ferry piled up economic, political, social, and religious responses all on its own. Brown, who was known to be a reader of Jonathan Edwards and a fervent Calvinist, hoped his effort would inspire slaves to seek their own liberty. He was universally noticed, but judged with sharply antithetical opinions.

In sum, even as from 1830 onward slavery slowly divided the nation, religion transformed division over slavery into a matter of ultimate concern.

Confusion between Slavery and Race

African Americans interpreted the events of the Civil War not as a statement about their conditions of servitude, but more directly as a statement about themselves.[33] So in April 1862 Bishop Daniel Alexander Payne preached to his Methodist congregation in Washington, D.C., to celebrate the newly enacted federal ban on slavery in the District. "Who has sent this great deliverance?" was Payne's query. "The answer shall be, the Lord; the Lord God Almighty, the God of Abraham and Isaac and Jacob." Only "Thou, O Lord, and thou alone couldst have moved the heart of this Nation to have done so great a deed for *this weak, despised and needy people!*"[34]

By contrast, most American whites did not view things the same way. If many whites could accept emancipation as a blow for freedom in the abstract, it is not clear what they thought of African Americans as people or as potential citizens. The disjunction between consideration of slavery and consideration of black people was a fixture in the nation's charged ideological history before, during, and after the War between the States. Yet it was a disjunction difficult to recognize at the time. Only rarely did commentators stop to consider what perhaps should have been obvious—and what now has been emphasized with unusual force in the work of Eugene Genovese and Elizabeth Fox-Genovese: that if race could have been taken out of the picture, some aspects of slavery may have offered a corrective to some aspects of America's economic acquisitiveness and social individualism.[35] Another possibility, much more congenial to modern observers, but which was almost as difficult to imagine in the nineteenth century, was that once the bonds of slavery were removed, the formerly enslaved would simply get on with life (as had happened for at least some former slaves in the ancient world), and with the same rights of citizenship as enjoyed by other citizens.

Neither of these logical possibilities—that American free-market capitalists could learn some positive lessons about community solidarity from some aspects of the institution of slavery, or that American freed slaves could simply become American citizens—had much of a chance in the nineteenth-century United States. On the eve of conflict in 1861, the reason was spelled out clearly by the émigré historian and theologian Philip Schaff when he wrote that *"the negro question lies far deeper than the slave question."*[36] Because solutions to economic and political problems of slavery differed from solutions to the social problems of race, repeated efforts by both whites and blacks to differentiate issues of slavery from issues of race exercised almost no influence. During Kentucky's acrimonious debate over a new state constitution in 1850, for example, one dissenting minister, John G. Fee, put matters about as clearly as they could be put. Fee was laboring against the biblical arguments that had been offered to defend slavery. He was exasperated. Even if, he countered, the New Testament did not condemn Roman enslavement of Teutons, Gauls, Greeks, and Egyptians, "What," he asked, "was the complexion of these nations?" His answer was that "most were as white or whiter than the Romans themselves." Consequently, Fee went on, if "the apostles' teaching and practice sanctioned slavery, it sanctioned *the slavery of the age*—the slavery amongst which the apostles moved. N.B. THIS SLAVERY WAS WHITE SLAVERY . . . the large portion of those enslaved were *as white, and many of them whiter than their masters."*[37]

A few others joined this chorus. Abraham Lincoln, for example, used part of a stump speech in Cincinnati in 1859 to explain why Stephen Douglas did not use the biblical arguments for slavery that so many of his Democratic supporters put forward. The reason? "Douglas knows that whenever you establish that Slavery was right by the Bible, it will occur that that Slavery was the Slavery of the *white* man—of men without reference to color."[38]

But it was African Americans who most aggressively stressed the incongruity of the fact that the American debate over slavery was simply assumed to be also a debate about race. As Frederick Douglass wrote in March 1861,

> nobody at the North, we think, would defend Slavery, even from the Bible, but for this color distinction. . . . Color makes all the difference in the application of our American Christianity. . . . The same book which is full of the Gospel of Liberty to one race, is crowded with arguments in justification of the slavery of another. Those who shout and rejoice over the progress of Liberty in Italy, would mob down, pray and preach down Liberty at home as an unholy and hateful thing.[39]

Yet, in the event, it proved quite easy both North and South to defend slavery from the Bible. Throughout the South and in many places of the North, it was widely assumed that since Scripture did not condemn the institution as such, it thereby sanctioned the form of black-only slavery that prevailed in the United States. Countless works—again arising almost as frequently in the North as in the South—casually transposed the terms "slaves" and "Africans" as if they were simply equivalent. If this was an entirely illogical move, it nonetheless arose from centuries of race prejudice that had made it intuitively certain for Caucasians of western European heritage both that slavery was limited to blacks and that all people of African descent were naturally prepared for slavery.

A few southerners, like George Fitzhugh, did carry the economic, social, and even biblical defense of slavery to the logical conclusion and propose slavery as an all-embracing social system in which members of all races might be enslaved. In this proposal the secular Fitzhugh was following where at least some religious voices had led. In 1837, for example, an anonymous "Traveling Preacher" proposed pan-racial slavery as a way to defend the "hireling" classes of the whole world against the brutalizing effects of industrial exploitation.[40] But the proposal to implement slavery for all races as a remedy for the contemporary abuse of labor was greeted with even less enthusiasm among whites than the observation that the slavery of Bible times was usually enslavement of Caucasians.

The result of this situation—where slavery had become the crux of national political development, where statements about slavery were confused with statements about the nature of African Americans, and where arguments about slavery had become irrevocably religious—was fraught with significance for the future. In the words of Genovese and Fox-Genovese, "This scripturally and intellectually weakest point in the biblical defense of slavery [that restricted slavery to blacks] emerged as the politically strongest. It gripped public opinion more firmly than any other. We live with the consequences of the ensuing tragedy."[41]

Even more compelling was the judgment of Frederick Douglass, which he rendered while the outcome of the war was still in doubt: "The law and the sword cannot abolish the malignant slaveholding sentiment which has kept the slave system alive in this country during two centuries. Pride of race, prejudice against color, will raise their hateful clamor for oppression of the negro as heretofore. The slave having ceased to be the abject slave of a single master, his enemies will endeavor to make him the slave of society at large."[42] To Douglass, the confusion between slavery and race was fatal, although even he could not guess how enduring the effects of that confusion would be.

The Civil War as a Religious Conflict

It does not require extensive elaboration to show that the Civil War—as a conflict to define the Union, determine the legitimacy of slavery, and specify the limits of states' rights—was also fundamentally a religious war fought over how to interpret the Bible and how to promote moral norms in national public life. This judgment was widely and regularly repeated during the conflict itself. So for the North, a sermon of thanksgiving in September 1864 that praised God for the success of Philip Sheridan in laying waste the Shenandoah Valley was entitled "The Bible Doctrine Concerning War." The assertions of the sermon were unequivocal: "We are upon Bible ground, therefore, when we invoke God in doing battle for a just cause, and we are following Biblical precedent when we ascribe to Him the victory. . . . The war which they [southerners] are waging upon the government of the United States is an unholy war, a monstrous conspiracy of crime."[43]

From the South, similar professions—though with the object of God's favor reversed—could be heard until very near the end. In the issue of the *Army and Navy Messenger for the Trans-Mississippi Department* published on March 16, 1865, for example, a die-hard held fast to his faith: "It is not often in the history of the world that such great crises,

involving the very fundamental elements of truth, conscience, and manhood, are allowed by Divine Providence
to occur. Such was the position of the Hebrew nation in
the midst of the Gentile world; such was the position of the
martyr church of Christ. . . . Such is our position now."[44]

The verdict that contradictory interpretations of the
Bible fundamentally affected the nature of the conflict
was clearly recognized by outside observers at the time. A
German editor wrote in 1863, for example, that "from the
perspective of the slave question," the War between the
States was "a formal war of religion."[45] This same conclusion has been echoed by modern historians who in recent
years have begun to explore the religious dimensions of the
conflict that had long, but inexplicably, remained under-
researched. James McPherson, as an instance, has recently
published significant materials supporting such conclusions,
as his own view that "Civil War armies were, arguably, the
most religious in American history."[46] On several fronts, a
growing number of historians are now pursuing research in
response to a broad challenge McPherson has posed: "Religion was central to the meaning of the Civil War, as the
generation that experienced the war tried to understand it.
Religion should also be central to our efforts to recover that
meaning."[47]

Religious beliefs and practices were not the *causes* of the
war in the way that dispute over the right of states with
respect to slavery was a cause. But they were everywhere an
overwhelmingly important context for the conflict. Those
who take up the challenge to measure the intensifying effects of religion on the outworking of the conflict do not
hesitate in their conclusions. Harry Stout is not the only one
who has suggested that "with unbroken confidence in God's
cause and no comment on [the morality of] man's conduct,

they [the clergy North and South] probably extended the war by a year—the bloodiest year as it turned out."[48]

The fact that religion was so central during the war was a direct result of how important religion had become before the war. Both northerners and southerners, hard-line abolitionists along with hard-line slavery advocates and the many who vacillated in between, almost all had looked for a word from God to resolve their dilemmas about slavery. Many had reached expressly for the written Word of God. This depth of religious conviction helps explain how the Republican administration in the North could succeed in its unprecedented expansion of centralized government authority, first to save the Union and then to exterminate slavery. It explains as well how the classically republican South, with its deep commitment to severely limited government, could allow the central Confederate state to become almost as vigorous as its northern counterpart. It was warfare that allowed deep-seated republican scruples to be set aside, but in this case it was warfare defined as work for the armies of the Lord.

⁓

The enduring problems bequeathed by antebellum controversies and by the Civil War itself can be summarized succinctly, however great the complexities to which these problems gave birth. The Civil War, because of principles espoused by radical Republicans and contingencies embraced by Abraham Lincoln, became a war to end slavery, rather than just to preserve the Union. Except for African Americans and a very few white Americans, however, it never became a war to overcome racism.

Before and during the Civil War, advocates on all sides eagerly deployed the Scriptures to defend their own convictions and skewer the convictions of their opponents. But this deployment was directed overwhelmingly to the question of slavery, only rarely to the question of race (even though the Bible is much clearer in its teachings against racism than it is about its permission of slavery).

Because this public use of the Bible was so prevalent, and also because religious convictions became so strong in support of war efforts North and South, the cause of the North and the cause of the South became religious matters of ultimate concern. In the process, both defending the nation and contending over slavery fed the creation of what Harry Stout has called "millennial nationalism as the primal religious faith."[49] At first this civil religion existed in two versions, one for the North and one for the South. But eventually, as national goals, legislation, and mythology successfully reunited the states, the nationalisms were also unified. Yet as David Blight and other historians have shown, the millennial patriotism and the civil religion that accelerated the reunion of North and South left little energy to address the festering problems of racial injustice.[50]

As a result, when the Civil War decisively settled the questions of national unity and slave legality, and when public religion became the servant of national civil religion, the public use of the Bible became much tamer than it had been before the war. There remained only a small and marginal interest, mostly expressed by African Americans, about what the Bible had to say about racism. And because African Americans were progressively deprived of a public voice in the decades after the war, national politics reflected scant influence from the only constituency that thought it was important to understand the Bible for its message on race as well as its implications for American national destiny.

CHAPTER II

The Origins of African-American Religious Agency

The political conflicts that led to the Civil War turned upon the question of slavery, and the question of slavery was always an intensely religious question. The kind of religion that energized debates over slavery was broadly Calvinistic, especially in its instinctive movement from biblical (or moral) principles to public actions; long after the specifics of Calvinist theology faded, that religious style remained a central feature of national public life. Yet despite a religious fixation on slavery during the antebellum and Civil War periods, religious confusion was the only result for consideration of race—before, during, and after that conflict. To show how broad patterns emblazoned on the national psyche by the crisis of the Civil War—interpreted as a religious and racial crisis as well as a political crisis—have shaped American politics to the present, the next two chapters carry the story of race, religion, and politics from the immediate postbellum years into the early twentieth century. The historical theme of these two chapters is the enduring effect of the Civil War.

This chapter makes a straightforward argument about the new epoch in African-American history opened by the war and the constitutional amendments that followed. The significance of that history was almost universally obscured as it was taking place; only after the unfolding of the civil rights movement has the great national importance of post-bellum black history—indeed, of postbellum black ecclesiastical history—begun to be realized. Even now, at this late date, the importance of what transpired in the black churches (from 1865 to 1925) for what transpired in the whole nation (from 1954 to 1968) has never received its due. This chapter makes a beginning by arguing for that importance.

The next chapter summarizes events in several national spheres. It treats the broad consequences that followed when, as a result of the Civil War, the evangelical religion of the antebellum period was unseated as a dominant force in *national* political life. Partly as a result of this religious reversal, the racial politics of the Civil War and its aftermath came to define frameworks for political-religious interaction, religious-racial interaction, and political-racial interaction from the 1860s until after World War I. Where evangelical religion proactively shaped national culture in the antebellum period, after the war religion of all kinds became the handmaiden of other ideologies. Only when the modern civil rights movement began to reconfigure the course of American political history did the kind of religious energy that had been so crucial for the whole of society during the antebellum years begin once again to shape the nation's moral and political agenda. By examining the long-term consequences flowing from the Civil War, these two chapters describe the thick web of continuities that brings the age of Nat Turner very close to the age of George W. Bush.

The effect of the Civil War that most directly influenced the nexus of race, religion, and politics was the opening of space for African Americans to create, direct, and manage their own churches and other institutions. While the full political effects of that opening would not be apparent until deep into the twentieth century, the energy displayed by blacks in the decades after the Civil War began a process that, decades later, would bring about a religious-inspired transformation of American public life. That energy was both organizational and intellectual.

Institutional Awakening

Organizationally, the Civil War was immensely significant for the opportunity it afforded African Americans to establish their own churches and educational activities, and also to create a literature for themselves. Church and school provided the foundation for the beginnings of a measure of African-American control over African-American destiny.[1] Even before the war was over, steps were being taken within previously existing northern denominations like the African Methodist Episcopal Church to expand into a liberated black South. From twenty thousand members in 1856, this denomination grew tenfold over the next two decades as it organized self-standing black churches in the former slave states.

As soon as the war was over, another kind of ecclesiastical organizing took place as former slaves began to establish new denominations—in 1865 the Colored Primitive Baptists of America; in 1866 a state convention for Baptists in North Carolina; in 1869 the Colored Cumberland Presbyterian Church; in 1870 the first general convention of the

Colored Methodist Episcopal Church that pulled together the work of five state conventions and witnessed the ordination of W. H. Miles and R. H. Vanderhorst as this important denomination's first black bishops. Links among state Baptist conventions developed later, but within a generation, by 1895, the National Baptist Convention came into existence to do for African-American Baptists what national organizations had done for African-American Methodists. Also before the end of the century, black holiness churches organized themselves as the Church of God in Christ (1897) under the leadership of C. H. Mason and C. P. Jones. The cooperation of Mason and Jones did not last long, but when they divided a few years later, the result was a powerful black Pentecostal denomination under Mason (the Church of God in Christ) and a major Holiness denomination for blacks under Jones (the Church of Christ [Holiness]).

Stride for stride alongside the emergence of black denominations came black educational institutions. At first with the extensive help of the Freedman's Bureau and of white Protestants from the northern denominations, but then under their own impetus, former slaves attended, patronized, founded, and expanded schools at every level, from night classes for literacy to colleges and universities. Among the latter, Howard (Washington, D.C.), Fisk (Nashville), and Storer (Harpers Ferry, W.Va.) were important institutions established with help from the North, while Lane (Jackson, Tenn.), Livingstone (Salisbury, N.Car), and Morris Brown (Atlanta) followed soon thereafter as creations by the black, mostly southern denominations. In the first years after the war, the newly organized or expanded churches and the educational institutions were joined by the Republican Party in providing opportunities for public black leadership. As Reconstruction was slowed and then overwhelmed by the reinstatement of racially exclusive white regimes, these opportunities were pulled back to churches, schools, and a very limited range of businesses serving an exclusively black clientele.

But even as white repression drove blacks back into the institutions they had themselves created and controlled, African-American publishing continued to expand.[2] Within a generation after the war, the denominations were sponsoring a wide range of religious publications, and they were joined by other purveyors of books and periodicals that explored national politics, advanced strategies for self-help, and offered consideration of Africa and the possibility of emigration, among many other topics. In and through the churches, therefore, and in broadening ripples from the churches, self-directed black organization began to emerge. In Eric Foner's well-considered judgment, "the creation of an independent black religious life proved to be a momentous and irresistible consequence of emancipation."[3]

Intellectual Revitalization

A key element in the emergence of black civil society was the strengthening of a distinctly African-American religious voice. In point of fact, there never was one African-American voice, but rather a distinctly African-American force field in which different religious expressions arose, merged, competed against each other, and provided an unusual measure of fruitful hybridization. This force field could be traced back into the early national and antebellum periods when African Americans, both slave and free, began to internalize Christian convictions and practices. The Christian beliefs that blacks accepted usually came from evangelical revivalism, but wherever they arose, they were contextualized in

African-American circumstances. Denominational leaders like Richard Allen of the AME Church and the Presbyterian Henry Highland Garnet stressed self-help and self-organization.[4] Various manifestations of "slave religion" existed further outside standard white boundaries but were already solidifying the religion that soon produced the black spirituals.[5] As they arose, these expressions of African-American Christianity almost always represented more than simply a duplication of white religion.

The difference after the Civil War was that the journey of ethical, moral, and theological reflection was becoming a journey of self-determination. The journey was not unrelated to earlier religious experience, but it was now out from under white control and free to develop its own trajectories. For a history of religious thought, narrowly considered, the black story from 1865 to about 1925 is one of increasing depth and diversification. For American history, broadly considered, the story is, again, one of apparent national irrelevance during wilderness years of preparation for a day of future opportunity.

Black religious thought in the generations after the Civil War moved on two levels, even as it moved in many directions. Those two were the realms of formal, elite discourse, and popular, lay-directed experience. The formal realm embraced several, not altogether harmonious, elements. Most prominent in the years surrounding the Civil War were strongly evangelical themes advocated by effective leaders like Bishop Daniel Alexander Payne, who after training at the Lutheran Gettysburg Theological Seminary became the leading bishop of the AME Church. Because Payne's evangelicalism drew on the same sources as the era's prominent white Protestant teachings, he was regularly moved to warn against "heathenish" practices he found among African Americans, like the ring shout with its "shouting, jumping, and dancing."[6] But Payne's strong evangelical convictions provided him and many others like him with a formidable depth of conviction and a formidable theological foundation.

Another active element in formal religious thought was Christian universalism, a theme that often emerged naturally with standard evangelical emphases. The Rev. William Christian, founder in 1889 of the Church of the Living God (Christian Workers for Fellowship), consistently preached that, since Jesus had no earthly father, he was "colorless" and belonged to all people.[7] The Rev. Elias Camp Morris, pioneering president of the National Baptist Association, joined Christian in asserting that the message of Christianity was for all people without differentiation everywhere: "The commission which [God] gives is without race, color or condition, but is that the gospel be preached to every creature. . . . 'Christ Jesus came into the world to save sinners,' not white sinners, nor black sinners, nor red sinners, but sinners."[8]

Francis Grimké regularly made this same appeal from his Presbyterian church in Washington, D.C., as when in 1916 he complained about the blind spots affecting much contemporary Protestantism. In reflecting on why the revivalist Billy Sunday had been so specific during a recent Washington campaign in denouncing some sins (drunkenness, sexual immorality) but not others (injustice, discrimination, economic oppression), Grimké paused to evaluate what it meant to be evangelized by such a message:

> The men and women who come into the church through these evangelistic efforts . . . have no more idea or intention of doing what Jesus wants them to do, except qualifiedly, than they have of butting their

heads against a stone wall. They come into the church and bring with them all their colorphobia. . . . Evangelism of that kind is of no real value. . . . Evangelism that is genuine . . . carries along with it brotherhood, that so presents Jesus Christ that men see, and see plainly, what is involved in accepting Him.[9]

Other elements that contributed to formal religious thought, like a strongly black emphasis, drifted further from standard evangelical themes. Henry McNeal Turner, who became a bishop in the AME Church after extensive military and political experience, wrote famously in 1896 that "God is a Negro," a claim meant to identify Christianity with outreach to subjugated populations. Turner's disillusionment with the course of affairs in the United States led him to explore African colonization and to establish ties with black churches in South Africa. He also complained that "the white man" had "colored the Bible in his translation to suit the white man, and made it, in many respects, objectionable to the Negro. And until a company of learned black men shall rise up and retranslate the Bible, it will not be wholly acceptable and in keeping with the higher conceptions of the black man. . . . We need a new translation of the Bible for colored churches."[10]

A strongly reformist element also shaped black religious thought, although reform could take many different shapes. Booker T. Washington, who promoted industrial vocational education; W.E.B. DuBois, who advocated intellectual and social self-assertion at the highest intellectual levels; and Marcus Garvey, a more secular proponent of emigration, could be harsh critics of each other.[11] But because they shared an eagerness to confront the forces that oppressed black people, their ideas were easily put to use by individuals representing a wide range of religious views.

By the early twentieth century, formal religious thought by African Americans had reached a relatively sophisticated level in a relatively short period of time. Among the masses of believing blacks, however, populist religious practice counted for more than formal intellectual effort. The strongly emotional and forthrightly physical practices that have been well described by Albert Raboteau, Sylvia Frey, Betty Wood, Eugene Genovese, and other scholars as marking antebellum black Christianity carried over broadly into the last decades of the nineteenth century.[12] Religious life defined by immediate contact with the divine, Bible knowledge keyed to miraculous interventions and self-sacrificing heroes, spirituals that rehearsed narratives of divine liberation—these and other well-established practices that had sustained African-American Christians in slavery continued to do so after emancipation.

When, near the turn of the century, W.E.B. DuBois visited rural black churches in the South, he described himself as a "school teacher . . . fresh from the East" who "had never seen a Southern Negro revival." DuBois found much to criticize in "the Preacher, the Music, and the Frenzy" of African-American worship, but also more than enough to convince him that "the Negro church of today is the social centre of Negro life in the United States, and the most characteristic expression of African character." Especially when he wrote about "the Frenzy"—which "varied in expression from the silent rapt countenance or the low murmur and moan to the mad abandon of physical fervor"—DuBois was opening up a world of remarkable religious depth and potential social force.[13]

By the start of the new century, Pentecostal practices were added in many places to this strong base of experiential religion. William Seymour, son of slaves and a well-traveled Holiness preacher who became the key promoter of the Azusa Street Pentecostal revivals of 1906, was a leader who, after internalizing the practices of "slave religion," had gone on to define a spiritual progression of justification followed by sanctification and then baptism in the Holy Spirit with speaking in tongues. His influence on fellow African Americans may not have been as great as it would become in the Christian world at large, but he was still an important bridge from nineteenth-century black spiritual practices to Pentecostal expressions of the twentieth century.

To Seymour's explicitly Christian influence should also be added the broad popular attention accorded to Father Divine and Bishop Charles Manuel (Sweet Daddy) Grace from the mid-1910s.[14] The Peace Mission of Father Divine and the United House of Prayer for All People of Sweet Daddy Grace were never accepted as fully orthodox Christian expressions, but their emphasis on multiracial worship and the ease with which they crossed the color line in a period of heightened race consciousness made them important promoters of a strongly integrationist element in popular black religion.

Stages of Development

The mixture that resulted from these currents of popular black religion, alongside currents of more formal, elite religious thought, did not yield a cohesive system. It was rather a potent brew of lively ingredients that had the potential of boiling over in several ways. Yet well into the twentieth century, the development of these black religious ideas seemed of little consequence for the populace in general. After World War II, their relevance for broader purposes became stunningly evident, and with a vengeance.

In passing, it is worth reflecting on the chronological parallels between the rise of evangelical Protestantism from the late eighteenth century to the Civil War and the emergence of black religion from after the Civil War to the 1960s. In both cases, small beginnings benefited from predecessors going before—for white evangelicals. the trans-Atlantic religious revivals of the mid-eighteenth century, and for blacks, the emergence of African-American Christianity in the early nineteenth century. In both, a first stage was marked by intellectual and organizational vitality leading to the creation of active and self-controlled institutions—for white evangelicals from about 1790 to 1820, for blacks from 1865 to the early in the next century. (In this perspective, what Stephen Marini has called "the Revolutionary revival" during the 1780s and 1790s corresponds to the flurry of spiritual and institutional expansion in the immediate wake of the Civil War.[15]) Then for both came a period of consolidation, continued recruitment, and initial exploration of public possibilities—from about 1820 to about 1840 for white evangelicals, and from the end of World War I to World War II for blacks. This initial exploration then gave way to a period of widespread public influence—for white evangelicals from about 1840 through the end of the Civil War, for blacks from after World War II into the 1970s. In both cases, wider American circumstances had much to do with the public influence exerted by these religious movements. But in each, a roughly parallel sequence of three generations—institutional creativity, intellectual deepening, public impact—marked the transition from a private religious movement with a narrow public presence to a public religious movement with a major effect on the political sphere.

Summary

As numerous scholars have now pointed out, broader developments in the nation obscured the significance of these African-American institutions. The retreat from Reconstruction, the unleashing of lynch-law terrorism, the general lack of concern for black civil rights in the North, and the imposition in the South of Jim Crow laws to quash black political participation seemed to neuter the nation's African-American population. The cri de coeur in 1900 of black novelist and social critic Pauline Hopkins reflected her dismay at the contemporary situation: "We thought that with the abolishment of slavery the black man's destiny would be accomplished. . . . [Yet today] a condition of affairs confronts us that [abolitionists] never foresaw: the systematic destruction of the Negro by every device which the fury of enlightened malevolence can invent. . . . This new birth of the black race is a mighty agony. God help us in our struggle for liberty and manhood!"[16]

W.E.B. DuBois offered a similar commentary on the current state of affairs when in 1905 he published the notes of the Declaration of Principles from the first meeting of the Niagara Movement. This organization, which held its founding gathering in a historic African-American church, Michigan Street Baptist in Buffalo, New York, was formed as an alternative to Booker T. Washington's incremental approach to improving race relations. DuBois lashed out in uncompromising terms: "The Negro race in America[,]

stolen, ravished and degraded, struggling up through difficulties and oppression, needs sympathy and receives criticism; needs help and is given hindrance, needs protection
and is given mob-violence, needs justice and is given char-
ity, needs leadership and is given cowardice and apology,
needs bread and is given a stone." Significantly, DuBois
offered further commentary in the form of a theological
judgment—"This nation will never stand justified before
God until these things are changed"—and an ecclesiastical
judgment—"Especially are we surprised and astonished at
the recent attitude of the church of Christ—on the increase
of a desire to bow to racial prejudice, to narrow the bounds
of human brotherhood, and to segregate black men in some
outer sanctuary."[17]

Yet Hopkins's testimony and DuBois's outburst, appear-
ing as they did in, respectively, a novel written by an African-
American for a literate African-American audience and an
articulate political manifesto from African Americans for
African Americans, were telling a story by how they expressed themselves as well as by what they said. Such commentary showed—as did also the Rev. Francis Grimké's
lectures in Washington during this same period—that be-
neath the level of national consciousness, black institutions
and black spokespeople were now sustaining a lively black
discourse for an expanding black audience. External conditions prevented that discourse from affecting the body
politic as a whole; in fact, political realities seemed to
threaten the viability of that discourse and the ones who
were producing it. But in only a short space of time, it had
been born, it had come into its own, and it was at least
surviving.[18]

CHAPTER III

The Churches, "Redemption," and Jim Crow

In broader historical perspective, the Civil War was as important for religion as for national politics. The evangelical Protestantism that had been such a dominant national force before the war certainly survived with considerable strength thereafter. But the era when evangelical priorities also dictated national priorities was over. When the Civil War showed evangelical Protestantism to be a force that could deepen social convictions and regional loyalties but could not harmonize social and regional antagonisms, the role of evangelical Protestantism in national politics, though still significant, moved from active to passive. A wide range of consequences followed.

Foundations for the Democratic Republic

To grasp the religious-political tectonics at work throughout American history, a rough schematization in terms of republican political theory is useful. From even before the United States came into existence, advocates of republicanism made almost as much of their fears as of their hopes. The republican hope was that a regime of checks and balances, of dispersed powers, of limited but responsible government, could avoid the tyranny that bedeviled Europe. The fear was that the populace would not maintain the moral character—in eighteenth-century terms, the virtue—without which even a republic was doomed to demagoguery and systemic injustice.

From the founding of the United States, national leaders had looked to religion as one of the most important guarantors of that moral character. George Washington in his Farewell Address of 1796 had provided a memorable statement of the conviction that religion was an indispensable prop for republican government: "Of all the dispositions and habits which lead to political prosperity, Religion and morality are indispensable supports.... 'Tis substantially true, that virtue or morality is a necessary spring of popular government. The rule indeed extends with more or less force to every species of free Government. Who that is a sincere friend of it, can look with indifference upon attempts to shake the foundation of the fabric?"[1]

But religion was not the only support that national leaders looked to for the success of republican government. A comparable security for the republic was sought in the democratic dispersal of authority to industrious citizens. As first articulated by Thomas Jefferson, and then in a more democratic form by Andrew Jackson, the expectation was that a healthy nation would result from leaving self-sufficient, white working men alone to freely cultivate opportunities for free labor and free trade. The ideal of the agrarian yeoman, and then of the free white citizen, seemed almost as important as the inner discipline of religion for the health of the republic.

The Founders were not disappointed. For the first generations of national history, religious voluntarism along with free labor and free trade did produce a flourishing democracy of remarkable strength.

Slavery and sectional controversy, however, created problems that could not be solved by voluntary religion, free markets, or free white men. The solution to these problems came, rather, from a central government acting with far more authority than even Alexander Hamilton had envisioned in proposing an active federal supervision of the new nation's fiscal affairs, or that the Whig Party had proposed in the 1830s and 1840s as a way of advancing national well-being. Among the many revolutionary aspects of the Civil War was the extent to which the federal government (and the Confederate government as well) expanded its power to accomplish large national tasks.

That broad exercise of central government authority did not, however, last long. With the retreat from Reconstruction by the late 1870s, market forces—largely untrammeled by religious concerns—came to dominate the American polity. To be sure, between the end of Reconstruction and the beginning of the New Deal, many proposals were advanced that would have authorized government to address national problems with national solutions. Progressives especially led the appeal for a national income tax, for federal restraints on business monopolies, for national legislation to regulate the labor of women and children, and for many other reforms to be administered from the center. World War I strengthened the appeal for a more active central government.

To these pragmatic and utilitarian appeals for a more active federal government, a moral force was added by a number of religious reformers who petitioned the national government to find solutions for national problems. These included the National Association to Amend the Constitution (in order to add God, Jesus, and the Bible to the Preamble), the National Reform Association, the Women's Christian Temperance Union, and the Anti-Saloon League.[2]

The Eighteenth, or Prohibition, Amendment of 1919 represented the most visible success of these appeals. To its advocates, the Eighteenth Amendment brought the right kind of coercive authority to the nation's most destructive problem. It thus represented a continuation of the expanded federal power intimated in the Thirteenth, Fourteenth, and Fifteenth amendments. But compared with either the Civil War era or the period after the Great Depression, the years from roughly 1876 to 1932 witnessed a relatively ineffective national government and a diffused rather than concentrated religious influence on national affairs. The failure of Prohibition to resolve the practical and moral problems of alcohol abuse testified to the relative superficiality of hopes for its success. That failure also testified to the relative superficiality of the reformist religion supporting the Eighteenth Amendment, and the relative weakness of the government that attempted to enforce it.

The federal government moved back decisively into the center of political life only with the New Deal. To address an economic crisis of unprecedented depth and duration, the federal government exerted unprecedented energies to meet the national emergency. By contrast to the period of the Civil War, once the immediate economic crises were met through the expansion of the federal government in the New Deal, central authority did not retreat. Rather the unfolding of World War II hard on the heels of the Depression and the New Deal, permanently directed national expectations toward national solutions for national problems.

TABLE 3.1
Changes in Primary Practical Support for American
Democratic-Republican Government

Years	Trend
1790–1860	Religion and market predominate; government latent
1860–1876	Government predominates; religion retreating; market rising
1876–1932	Market predominates; religion latent; government indecisive
1932–1954/55	Government and market predominate; religion latent
1954/55–present	Government, market, and religion compete for predominance

Not until after World War II did religion once again attain the national prominence it had exercised in the decades before the Civil War. The vehicles for that prominence were civil rights reforms and conservative movements quickened to life at least partly in reaction to those reforms. Thus, once religion did again begin to assert national influence, it was a fractured presence driving public life in contradictory directions, even though the two strongest national religious forces—as expressed, first, in the civil rights movement and then in the New Religious Right—were both descended from the evangelical religion that had been such a dominant force in the antebellum period.

Table 3.1 charts U.S. history in terms of the forces or agents that were most active in various periods to support the ongoing experiment of democratic republicanism.

The Political Weakening of Evangelical Religion

The exigencies of warfare and Reconstruction explain why the federal government became the nation's dominant political force from 1860 to 1876. But from a religious standpoint, there is more to be said. Evangelical Protestantism lost out in national political influence because, while it had the strength to animate the division over slavery, it did not display the political wisdom required to resolve the issue of slavery or the political strength to unify the halves of the nation divided by war over slavery.[3]

American national culture had been built in substantial part by evangelicals who exploited voluntary and democratic means to internalize the message of Scripture as they understood it, to organize themselves for purposeful action, and to spread Christian revivalism as a redeeming and organizing force in the land. Yet in the run-up to the Civil War, democratic and voluntary uses of the Bible had led to an impasse. The voluntaristic and scriptural means that evangelicals had employed to create the national culture faltered before the unbridgeable chasm of opinion about what the Bible actually taught concerning slavery.

Only because religious belief and practice had become such powerful civilizing forces before the conflict, only because they had done so much to create the nation that went to war, did that conflict result in such a great alteration in the influence of religious belief and practice on the nation. In the wake of the conflict, two great problems confronted the churches: one was the enduring reality of racism, which displayed its continuing force almost as virulently through the mob and the rope as it had in the chain and the lash. The other was the expansion of consumer capitalism, where unprecedented opportunities to create wealth were matched by large-scale alienation and new depths of poverty in both urban and rural America. For religion to have addressed these two problems constructively, America's believers needed the kind of intellectual and institutional vigor that evangelical Protestants had brought to bear on so many tasks in the generations between the Revolution and the Civil War.

Instead, the Civil War was won and slavery was abolished not by religious agency, but by an unprecedented expansion of central government authority and by a hitherto unimaginable degree of industrial mobilization. If the war freed the slaves and gave African Americans a constitutional claim to citizenship, it did not provide the moral energy required for rooting equal rights in the subsoil of American society or for planting equal opportunity throughout the land. If the war showed what could be accomplished through massive industrial mobilization, it did not offer clear moral guidance as to how that mobilization could be put to use for the good of all citizens.

To be sure, the evangelical Protestant traditions that had done so much to shape society before the war were not rendered powerless in its wake. Yet they were now much more deeply divided than before. North vs. South and black vs. white represented only two of such divisions. The nation's evangelical phalanx was now also riven between populist, lay-driven energies of the sort displayed by Dwight L. Moody, the era's leading urban evangelist, and the academic, formal energies of the sort found at the nation's first-rank colleges, which had begun to absorb evolutionary and higher critical conceptions of religion from Europe's elite intellectuals. The beliefs and practices that were so prominent nationally in the antebellum period did remain important after the war for millions of individuals, within networks dominated by the churches, and in many local regions. But because those beliefs and practices had not been able to resolve the issue of slavery, which had torn the nation apart, and because they were divided in meeting the practical and intellectual challenges that burgeoned after the war, they gave way in national influence to the expansion of federal power and the exercise of market forces that dominated the political landscape for the next two generations.

Benefits of Expanded Religious Space

For the general practice of religion, the receding national authority of British-origin evangelical Protestants was a good thing. When this formerly dominant family of denominations lost predominant influence over national public life, it opened space for other religious communities to flourish in specific localities and to begin to be accepted as "Americans." Some evangelicals, like the Episcopalian political theorist Elisha Mulford and the Congregational social Christian Josiah Strong, did continue to argue for a distinctly Protestant nation and were not at all shy about fomenting opposition to Catholics, Jews, and other non-Protestants on that basis.[4] But in the postbellum decades, such arguments were easily turned aside; they never led to the kind of political influence that had been won by the strongly anti-Catholic American (or Know-Nothing) Party in elections from the mid-1850s. Rather, in Isaiah Berlin's categories, religious liberty in the United States after the Civil War moved decisively in the direction of "negative freedom," which describes the new situation where most groups were allowed to get on with the work of building their own communities, and away from "positive freedom," which prevailed during the antebellum period when evangelicals tried to shape the

American public sphere into their idea of a godly republic. So it was that Protestants not of British origin, Roman
Catholics, Jews, Eastern Orthodox, free-thinking secularists,
and a host of smaller religious bodies began to be genuinely
at home in the land of the free. The complicated maneuvers
by which the Mormons adjusted their earlier practice of
polygamy as the price for nearly unlimited liberty to fashion a Latter-day Saints culture in Utah illustrated the
space that more and more nonevangelical groups were winning in more and more regions of the country.[5] Significantly,
and despite the desire of some in the white evangelical denominations, the evangelical inability to dominate Lutherans, Catholics, Jews, and Mormons was mirrored in the
white evangelical inability to dominate the black churches.

The Rise and Rapid Fall of Central
Government Authority

With the relative decline of evangelical Protestantism as a
national public force, the central government for a brief period became the dominant influence in the nation's public
life.[6] During the war itself, the unprecedented demands of
conflict pushed the northern Republican Party reluctantly,
and Confederates of all stripes even more reluctantly, to accept an ever-expanding role for the national state. After the
end of the conflict, a muddle ensued until congressional Republicans seized control of Reconstruction from President
Andrew Johnson, whose sympathies lay with white southern
leaders who desired a speedy return to the status quo antebellum. Those sympathies were expressed in traditional
small-r republican warnings against the threat of unchecked

national power. But under congressional Reconstruction, the national government put troops on the ground in the South, coordinated the efforts of northern and southern voluntary agencies (many of them evangelical) who provided education and economic assistance to freed slaves, and taxed the whole country to pay for this exercise of national authority.

So long as central government retained the capacity to act nationally, it was conceivable that the abolition of slavery accomplished by the Thirteenth Amendment (1865) would go on to address the even more difficult task of guaranteeing civil rights for citizens of all races. The Fourteenth Amendment (1868) announced such a guarantee as applicable to all persons born in the United States, including former slaves. It boldly proclaimed that no state was "to make or enforce any law which shall abridge the privileges or immunities of citizens"; and it decreed that no state was to "deprive any person of life, liberty, or property, without due process of law; nor deny to any person within its jurisdiction the equal protection of the laws."

Shortly thereafter, the Fifteenth Amendment of 1870 went even further to guarantee the right to vote for all male citizens regardless of "race, color, or previous condition of servitude." Earlier, the Fourteenth Amendment had even spelled out in considerable detail the extensive penalties that would fall on states "when the right to vote at any election for the choice of Electors for President and Vice-President of the United States, Representatives in Congress, the executive and judicial officers of a State, or the members of the legislature thereof, is denied to any of the male inhabitants of such State . . . or in any way abridged, except for participation in rebellion, or other crime."

For the brief span of years during which these amendments were approved, it seemed that a vigorous national government might therefore accomplish what antebellum exertions from the informal establishment of evangelical voluntarists had not been able to accomplish. The evangelical denominations and voluntary associations had made some efforts to translate the Bible's message of universal dignity for all humanity into the functioning practices of the land, but now the government itself seemed to secure a variation of that promise in the Constitution. Especially as African-American men began to exercise the franchise and when a few African Americans were voted into statewide and national office, it seemed as if the determined actions of central government against racism might begin to match the effectiveness of central government action against slavery.

But national willingness to support an active national government failed. Already the presidential election of 1868 was a harbinger, when the Democratic candidate Horatio Seymour of New York won more than 47% of the popular vote against the war's lionized military hero, Ulysses S. Grant, and at a time when military occupation gave Republicans a virtual lock on several states in the former Confederacy. Seymour's pledge to remove the federal presence from the former Confederacy as rapidly as practicable met with almost as much approval in the North as in the South.

By the early 1870s, the emergence in the Republican Party of a "liberal" faction (meaning, in nineteenth-century terms, a small-government faction) indicated a growing uneasiness about prosecuting Reconstruction vigorously. This almost exclusively northern movement reflected small-r republican reservations about the corrupting influence of big government, influence that in critical states like New York seemed all too evident in the machinations of Democratic machine politics. Republican Party "liberalism" also reflected the growing influence of businessmen who either during or shortly after the war had embarked on the rapid industrialization of the American economy. To such ones, an active federal government was both dangerous politically and obstructive economically. The political trajectory of liberal Republicanism was indicated by the movement of Horace Greeley, longtime editor of the New York *Tribune* and the Democratic-Liberal Republican candidate for president in 1872. Greeley began as a crusader who advocated Negro rights and supported Reconstruction; he ended as a conservative who warned against black "dependency" and opposed President Grant's exercise of federal authority in the North as well as in the South. Currents within the northern Republican Party were working against the principle of aggressive national agency that represented the only hope for the South to transform emancipation into full civil rights.[7]

Simultaneously, the process that white southerners called "redemption," whereby white supremacists regained control of state governments in the former Confederacy, was also well under way. Here the story involved another reassertion of republican fears that accompanied decisive maneuvers by the white population and the Democratic Party, both of which had been marginalized by black emancipation and federal Reconstruction. The process also involved the brutal application of naked terror. The graphic example of Mississippi leading up to the congressional elections of 1874 and then in the election seasons of 1875 and 1876 became an inspiring template for other aggrieved white Democrats throughout the South.[8] These critical elections were accompanied by several pitched battles between Democratic militias and Republican forces loyal to Mississippi's elected government; many isolated bushwackings, murders, and executions; and a great tide of threat, beating, intimidation, and economic coercion. Against this violence, President Grant at first offered tentative assistance to the Republican-led Mississippi government. Then when the GOP's defense of Reconstruction became less politically advantageous than establishing its reputation for "reform," the federal assistance dried up.

Meanwhile, a whirlwind of political rhetoric constantly reiterated the republican themes of corruption, unchecked central authority, and despotism. Senator L.C.Q. Lamar of Mississippi was regarded as a moderate Democratic, but in a letter from the mid-1870s he articulated harshly the message that drove "redemption" in the South and won it a measure of respect in the North: "Draw a line on one side of which you see property, intelligence, virtue, religion, self-respect, enlightened public opinion, and exclusion from political control; and on the other the absolute unchecked political supremacy of brute numbers, and there you will behold not one attribute of free government, but the saddest & blackest tyranny that ever cursed the earth."[9]

Southern "redemption" represented a counterrevolution. It involved the violent transfer of power from liberated slaves and their Republican allies to an all-white Democratic Party. Significantly for the ideological conventions that dominated national politics into the mid-twentieth century, "redemption" also forged a strong bond between southern local control of racial matters and a rhetoric that pictured the exertion of national government authority as tyrannical, corrupt, and ungodly. The success of "redemption" fixed for the whole nation the pairing of local autonomy and racial exclusion as triumphant over the pairing that Nicholas Lemann succinctly labeled "black political empowerment and federal authority."[10]

In sum, the door that the Civil War had opened to full political participation by all citizens, black as well as white, was rapidly closing.

The election of 1876 and its aftermath sealed the retreat from active Reconstruction. In that disputed election, the Republican Rutherford B. Hayes of Ohio gained the White House, despite receiving 3% fewer popular votes than his Democratic opponent, Samuel J. Tilden of New York. Tilden had campaigned aggressively for a pull-back of federal authority in all areas of national life. Where former Confederate states had been returned to local control, Tilden swept to victory, as he did in winning 108 electoral votes from nine Union states (Connecticut, Delaware, Indiana, Kentucky, Maryland, Missouri, New Jersey, New York, and West Virginia). But in three former Confederate states where significant numbers of blacks still voted and significant numbers of ex-Confederates were still kept from the polls (Florida, Louisiana, South Carolina), and for one of Oregon's three electoral votes, the popular totals were too close to determine a clear winner. A federal commission, which ignored both the violent intimidation that had kept blacks from the polls throughout the South and what probably were narrow victories for Tilden in the disputed states, gave the contested electoral vote to Hayes. In return, the Republicans agreed to an end of congressionally mandated Reconstruction, which led immediately to the withdrawal of troops from the former Confederacy, and also agreed to return state governments in Louisiana, Florida, and South Carolina to the hands of ex-Confederate white leaders.

Race and Religion, South and North

The national unwillingness to maintain support for an active central government opened the way, once again, for race and religion to act together with powerful political effects, but this time negatively, as promoters of social passivity, instead of positively, as promoters of social activism. The reasons for the failure of Reconstruction, and with it the failure to move beyond the elimination of slavery to the guarantee of civil rights for all Americans, are well known. Full-scale support for Reconstruction from an active central government appeared to violate deeply ingrained republican instincts about the dangers of large government. More specifically, southern white racism proved stronger than the federal defense of civil rights. But it was not just the South. The will of integrationists from all sections of the country was undermined, either by new causes that drew attention away from race, by weariness in pursuing the very difficult goals of legal and social equality, by visions of spirituality that downplayed worldly involvements, or by violence.

In the South

The role of vigilante violence in winning the white South a victory in peace that its armies could not gain in war has been the subject of a cascade of scholarship on lynching and the other physical means used to disenfranchise blacks and restore control of southern society to racist governments.[11] In that literature, a prominent theme is the use of mob violence to defend the virtue of white women and the sanctity of the white Christian home against the depredations of black sexual assault. These violent measures, adopted as they were to defend white sexual purity, may reflect the most irrational moment in all of American history, since the ubiquity of lighter-skinned African Americans testified continually and unmistakably to the many generations of sexually predatory acts by white males upon black women.

This domestic rallying point for white concern also recalled a parallel situation from an earlier time. As Christopher Hill once pointed out, English Puritanism may be said to have taken shape in the late sixteenth century *after* reform-minded Church of England Calvinists lost the struggle to remodel their national church.[12] In response, Hill suggests, Puritans turned to the domestic sphere—the only sphere they still controlled—as the focus for their reforming efforts. The result was a burst of religious energy that created the Puritan Sabbath, led to an intense devotional revolution transcribed in spiritual diaries, and prompted a distinctly Puritan practice of conversion—but only after Puritan energies had been diverted from earlier efforts to reform the whole nation. The parallel to the postbellum South is that the white population, having lost the war, turned to exert control over the domestic sphere as the only sphere in which it could act without federal interference. The difference between the two situations was, however, as great as the similarity. The Puritan turn inward generated a dynamism that has influenced English-speaking Protestants to this day, as a model both for spirituality and eventually for how a dissenting and marginalized religious movement may exert influence in the public square. A similarity with the postbellum South is that white efforts to control the domestic sphere also eventually resulted in great influence in the public sphere. The great contrast is that white southern reaction to the loss of public authority as a result of the Civil War led to a flourishing of racist practices that have never influenced spiritual or social development anywhere else in the world.

Along with the willingness to use extralegal violence, a widespread willingness to exploit the resources of traditional evangelical religion also drove opposition to Reconstruction and played an important part in bringing central government action to a halt. On the religious factors in what was called at the time the "redemption" of the South, a number of authors have made outstanding recent contributions.[13] Together, these historians have demonstrated that religion, in the North as well as the South, was critical in the process that brought Reconstruction to a close, restored white racist regimes to power, and turned the attention of the North away from defending citizens' rights for all.

Religiously inspired actions were usually passive, as pastors and church leaders stood by silently while the Ku Klux Klan, the Knights of the White Camellia, and other organized mobs menaced, assaulted, or murdered African Americans who attempted to take up the opportunities guaranteed by the Thirteenth, Fourteenth, and Fifteenth amendments, and the whites who, however cautiously, supported their efforts. Occasionally church leaders could be more active, as when John Ezell, a Baptist minister in Spartanburg County, South Carolina, joined the local Klan in mob actions against white and black Republicans, only to repent before a court with an admission that he "did not believe he was safe outside of the klan."[14] During the early 1870s, the wife of Mississippi's Republican governor reported to relatives in the North that the state's ministers used their Sunday sermons to encourage disloyalty to the Union.[15]

In later decades, influential religious leaders either simply accepted "redemption" or provided it active support. A particularly telling incident was the response of revivalist Sam Jones to the 1899 lynching and mutilation of Sam Hose, which took place in Georgia during the nadir of that state's lynching frenzy.[16] At the time Jones was the South's most famous itinerant preacher, who also enjoyed a national reputation for his salty, straightforward preaching of homespun Christian morality. Hose was a farm laborer accused of murdering his employer and raping the employer's wife in an incident that probably involved violent provocation

from the employer. Shortly afterwards, Jones publicly pro-
tested against the lynching as a breach of regular judicial
procedure. But then when white opponents defended the
act as a Christian defense of the home and of sexual purity, Jones shifted his stance and himself became a defender
of what had happened. In this incident, the independent-
mindedness for which Jones was famous as a preacher
was of no avail in standing against the religious, as well as
sociopolitical, conventions of his day. Whether actively or
passively, white southern religion all but unanimously supported the imposition of white supremacist rule and for a
very long time offered scant resistance to its continuation.

In the North

From the North, the willingness of well-known public
religious figures like the evangelist Dwight L. Moody,
the preacher Henry Ward Beecher, the novelist Harriet
Beecher Stowe, or the temperance advocate Frances Willard to sacrifice black civil rights to other religious goals
made their own important contribution to the "redemption" of the South.[17] Moody was a close friend of General
O. O. Howard, the head of the Freedman's Bureau after
whom Howard University in Washington, D.C., was named,
and he had been inclined during his years in Chicago to act
with considerable fairness toward African Americans. But
when, in 1876, he conducted a preaching campaign in
Augusta, Georgia, and local white leaders insisted upon
segregating the audience, Moody reluctantly gave in to
their wishes.[18] Until the mid-1890s, and despite a willingness to speak before black audiences, Moody maintained a
policy of segregation for his meetings.

This general pattern was widespread. Despite the ex-
tremes of his wartime rhetoric against the Confederacy,

Henry Ward Beecher after the war became an advocate of southern home rule and an opponent of federal authority to enforce Reconstruction.[19] When Harriet Beecher Stowe began, in the 1870s, to spend winters in Florida, she rapidly came to advocate sectional reconciliation and white supremacy.[20] For her part, Frances Willard led the Women's Christian Temperance Union to accept newer patterns of segregation and also joined the "liberal Republican" chorus in favoring voting restrictions for both southern blacks and northern immigrants.[21] In general, and with only a few exceptions, influential Protestant leaders in the North came to place much more emphasis on sectional reconciliation than on the continued fight against racial discrimination.

In this effort they were caught up in a major consequence of the War between the States. The war effort had encouraged views of providence that fixed on the divine calling of the United States as an extraordinary national agent of world-historical importance. For example, Horace Bushnell, often regarded as the nation's most creative theologian of the mid-nineteenth century, spoke at the Yale commencement in July 1865 and gave expression to his sense of the reunited nation's God-given destiny. To Bushnell, the war, as by a miracle from God, had brought about a form of national unity unthinkable before it began. The source of the unity was clear: "It will be no more thought of as a mere human compact, or composition, always to be debated by the letter, but it will be that bond of common life which God has touched with blood; a sacredly heroic, Providentially tragic unity, where God's cherubim stand guard over grudges and hates and remembered jealousies, and the sense of nationality becomes even a kind of religion."[22]

By contrast, some whites and many blacks pointed to the end of slavery and full citizenship for all African Americans as an even clearer demonstration of providential action. But as fixation on national providence grew stronger, only African Americans continued to reflect on the providence that ended slavery.[23] Especially when belief in national providence became a filter through which to view the divine right of the United States as a colonial power in the Caribbean and the Philippines, confidence in providence did little to challenge the nation's racist mores. It was not necessarily logical for national leaders to assert for American audiences the republican equation between unchecked national power and corruption high and low, while at the same time invoking God's blessing on the expansion of U.S. political power overseas. But in the last years of the century, this conjunction spoke for the era's strongest ideological, political, and economic commitments.

The result for religion of this providential interpretation of destiny was what David Blight has described for the nation as a whole: North-South reconciliation trumped efforts to reform racial attitudes and practices in all regions of the country and left African Americans, even the hundreds of thousands who had fought in the Union armed forces, on their own in the face of local prejudice and discrimination.[24]

Among Evangelicals

To the extent that D. L. Moody's type of evangelical religion represented widespread beliefs, it also contributed to racial difficulties. More in reflecting than in leading the white evangelical spirit of his age, Moody, as if in conscious reaction to the political overcommitments of evangelicals during and after the Civil War, guided his audiences away from external and social duties toward a consideration of inner and personal states of being. Along with large segments of the Protestant world, Moody's heightened stress on personal piety seemed to entail a decrease of interest in social conditions. Innovative groups like the Salvation Army were an exception, as the Army marshaled its strong Holiness piety to promote aggressive social service. But Moody and his supporters were representative of a wide swath of northern Protestant religion in speaking much about evil reflected in sins of the flesh, little about sins of greed, and almost nothing about sins of social domination.

The late nineteenth century also witnessed increasing efforts by other Protestants, north and south, to mine the Bible for its prophecies about the future. In earlier periods of Christian history, such a fixation had been pursued alongside use of the Bible for its prophetic messages about the present. For example, the Puritan pastor Cotton Mather had been both an ardent millennialist and an ardent social reformer. That earlier combination did not, however, prevail at the end of the nineteenth century. Then it seemed a case of either the Bible for the future or the Bible for the present. At least one historian of popular religion in the South has traced a connection between the apocalyptic fixation driving the prophecy emphasis and the Manichean insistence on black-white racial divisions.[25] The end result from shifting theological emphases toward the turn of the century was that the more conservative and pietistic elements of American Protestantism were neutering the social impact of Christian faith even as many evangelicals continued to find manifold resources in traditional Christianity for private devotion and domestic guidance.[26]

Among Progressives

The more progressive segments of the Protestant world that did retain an interest in social justice did not always include racial matters in these concerns. Notable social reformers

who otherwise exerted unusual efforts at embodying biblical values in their reforms regularly turned aside from racial
problems. William Jennings Bryan, the era's most consis-
tent political Christian, may have hinted at the need to address racial injustice, but those hints were overwhelmed by
his need to maintain good relations with the Democratic
power base in the South. Especially as Jim Crow hardened
during Bryan's repeated campaigns for president, he ac-
ceded more and more to external realities and so paid less
and less attention to African Americans. In the judgment
of Michael Kazin, who quotes a contemporary critic of
the Democratic Party, its "'overpowering, localized, negro
problem' gave the lie to Bryan's attacks on the haughty,
selfish policies of the GOP—a flaw the candidate himself
never understood."[27]

The Social Gospel movement of the late nineteenth and
early twentieth centuries did include a few figures who consistently struggled for racial transformation. Among them
the midwestern Congregational minister Harlan Paul Douglass, author in 1909 of *Christian Reconstruction in the South*,
was the most active opponent of the nation's ingrained pattern of racial discrimination.[28] But for the most part, leaders
of the Social Gospel focused their attention on problems
of urban poverty and class alienation among whites rather
than on racial injustice.

Walter Rauschenbush, the movement's most profound
theologian, was representative. He saw much in American society that needed the rebuke of Christian reform,
but he felt no particular urgency in challenging the era's
conventions about race. For Rauschenbush, the sad plight
of African Americans would be rectified by the same sort
of economic improvements and Christianizing impulses
that he felt were improving the circumstances of at least

some immigrant communities.[29] From all sides of the well-established American Protestant world, in other words, came silence, complicity, or active assistance to the "redemption" of the South.

Among Catholics

Religious cooperation with the imposition of Jim Crow laws in the post-Reconstruction South extended, however, beyond the Protestant world. Historically, the American Catholic Church had never been as concerned about questions of race and slavery in themselves as they were about how race and slavery affected integration into American society and the church's ability to maintain its internal unity along with ties to Rome.[30] Broader patterns of Catholic interaction with the political environment had determined Catholic positions on slavery during the Civil War era and strongly influenced Catholic attitudes toward race deep into the twentieth century.

The early history of Catholics in the United States was defined by the daunting task of making their way in an American nation that had been founded by largely Protestant interests and in which a strong revival of evangelical Protestantism was under way since the early nineteenth century. In this setting, the American church tried to provide cohesion and stability for its relatively small number of traditional adherents as well as for the great burgeoning of Irish and German immigrants who poured into the country from the 1840s. Within the large population of Catholic immigrants, the Irish were warned off abolition because of its British and nativist associations, while Germans reacted against the abolitionism, liberalism, and anticlericalism of the European supporters of the 1848 Revolutions, who had also migrated to America in great numbers. For this constituency, the church's main goals were conservative: to achieve social stability for its often impoverished adherents, religious stability through the promotion of traditional Catholic teaching, and cultural stability through its opposition to radicalism and revolution.

And they had to do so while always conscious of hostile or suspicious evangelical, reforming, and nativist forces. These forces had come to the surface dramatically in the career of the American Party (known popularly as "Know-Nothings") that in the mid-1850s rode its anti-immigrant, anti-Catholic stance into brief political prominence. Moreover, of all "Yankee" reforms, abolition was the most radical for its potential to disrupt social order and threaten communal unity. Given these American dynamics, Catholics were pushed ineluctably toward the Democratic Party. Although this party also harbored some evangelical and nativist elements, it was organized to protect local interests, especially the interests of slaveholders in the South.

American clerics did attempt to promulgate traditional Catholic teachings on slavery, which had never considered slaveholding a sin, but which did include strict guidelines for humanizing the institution by protecting slave marriages, demanding slave religious instruction, and maintaining the mass as a rite to which all (black and white) were called for common worship. The apostolic letter *In Supremo* (1839) from the very conservative Pope Gregory XVI pointed the way with its strong denunciation of the slave trade and its strict instructions about humane treatment of the enslaved. In addition, a traditional wariness about unrestrained capitalism came into play when the church criticized the notion of chattel slavery (treating humans as objects) and the lust for profit that seemed to drive American society as a whole, including the slave system.

If, however, Catholic teaching offered a powerful, if moderate, voice against the abuses of slavery, that voice never exerted much influence on the Catholic faithful because of the particulars of the American environment. Rather, Catholics remained more concerned about the threat of radical reform than the abuses of the slave system. When President Lincoln's Emancipation Proclamation (January 1, 1863) announced the manumission of slaves in the Confederacy, even most northern Catholics were only tepid in their support. No Catholic came out four-square for abolition until the Civil War was well under way. And especially Irish Catholics were key participants in riots and other violent resistance to the slavery reforms promoted by the Republican Party. After the war, while the bishops maintained their position of apolitical conservatism, lay voices spoke out forcefully against passage of the Thirteenth, Fourteenth, and Fifteenth amendments.

Also after the war, especially lower-class Catholics, often Irish, who were economic competitors with liberated slaves, found themselves pulled along when the Democratic Party allied itself with the Ku Klux Klan and other racist movements to strip blacks of their newly won civil rights. In these circumstances, it was a short step for some Catholics to move from a religiously based ideological anti-abolitionism to a racially grounded opposition to black civil rights. In Michael Hochgeschwender's careful phrase, "Antiradical perception of political enemies and racism defined the practical stance of Catholics in relationship to the freed slaves."[31]

Eventually, this general Catholic position also came to prevail in the unusual racial configuration of Louisiana. As James Bennett has shown in his superb study of New Orleans, Louisiana Catholics long displayed an unusual flexibility on race, with an unusual triracialism—blacks, whites,

creoles—that moderated at least some of the nation's stri-
dent biracialism.[32] By the end of the nineteenth century,
however, the Catholic Church in New Orleans began to
bring its traditional racial flexibility into line with the nation's hardening racial categories. In the mid-1890s—at
the very time when the Supreme Court ruled against a
Louisiana Creole in *Plessy v. Ferguson* and sanctioned the
segregationist regime of "separate but equal"—Catholics
in New Orleans opened their first church designated for
blacks only. Over the next two decades, the forces that
had led Louisiana's large Methodist population to sanction
Jim Crow discrimination also came to prevail in the state's
Catholic churches.

The important point to be made about Reconstruction re-
peats what had been true as well for the Civil War. Just as
the depth and intensity of antagonism in that war had been
a product, in substantial part, of religious conviction, so too
did religion figure crucially, and in many ways, to propel the
national retreat from federally sponsored Reconstruction.
The "redemption" of the South was, as the name suggests, a
spiritual turning point, as well as a political turning point.

Unperceived at that time but now visible because of
recent historical scholarship is the depth of ironic pathos
revealed by the use of the term "redemption" to describe
the recovery of white racist political power. More than a
century before 1876, Jupiter Hammon, a slave from Long
Island, had brought to print the very first work ever published by an African American. It was a long poem with the
title "An Evening Thought: Salvation by Christ, with Peni-
tential Cries." The first stanza of this first African-American

publication featured themes, vocabulary, and a fixation on the Bible that were all central to the forces that in the 1870s turned back, or turned aside from, Reconstruction. But although it could not have been recognized at the time, the themes of the poem were also continuing to resonate in black churches as well:

> Salvation comes by Jesus Christ alone,
> The only Son of God;
> Redemption now to every one,
> That loves his holy Word.[33]

As hard as it would have been to imagine in the post-Reconstruction decades, the day would once again come when Jupiter Hammon's sense of "redemption" would once more rival the anti-Reconstruction use of the word.

Domains of Continuing Religious Strength

It is important to be clear about the fate of religion in the late-nineteenth-century United States. When the evangelical Protestant phalanx receded as a dominant force in national politics after the Civil War, it did not mean that religion as a whole went into decline. To the contrary, religious energies may actually have been increasing during this period, but in diverse forms pushing in uncoordinated directions. Roman Catholics were growing stronger in many urban areas of the East, and in some of the western states, though this organization was still a few years removed from when Catholics would venture boldly into the national political arena. Catholics were joined—though in smaller numbers and over less territory—by other religious bodies that also were advancing from strength to strength. These bodies included Lutherans in the upper Midwest, Mormons in Utah, Hispanic Catholics in the Southwest, and what could be called the "Methodist belt" that stretched from Delaware to Kansas.

The strongest regional concentration of a specific religious tradition was, however, the former Confederate South, as recorded by the 1890 census. The Civil War that broke the national power of evangelical Protestant movements of British origin enabled those same movements to exert a new kind of hegemony throughout the southern region of the country. With the exception of Louisiana and its Catholic communities, the religious affiliations of the other ten states recorded extraordinary majorities for the Methodists and Baptists, who might have fought each other like cats and dogs, but only as an expression of what Freud called "the narcissism of small differences."[34] Thus, in 1890 Methodists and Baptists made up over 90% of the churched population in Georgia and Mississippi; over 80% in Alabama, Arkansas, North Carolina, South Carolina, and Virginia; and at or over 70% in Florida, Tennessee, and Texas.[35] (See table 3.2.) The concentration of Baptists was especially important for ideology, since this was the American religious tradition with the strongest fears about outside influence from top-down national elites and the strongest commitment to the Christian faith understood as a personal, rather than social, force. These religious convictions merged easily with political fears of an intrusive national government and political commitment to the prerogatives of local government.

The religious transformation brought on by the Civil War actually solidified the place of the more or less sectarian evangelical bodies in the former Confederate states, even as it defused evangelical influence in the nation as a whole. The effect of these developments on political life

TABLE 3.2
Baptist and Methodist Proportions of Church Populations, 1890
(by state)

A. Baptist Proportion of Church Population

Confederate South	Percentage
Virginia	53.3
Georgia	52.6
Mississippi	52.2
Alabama	46.2
North Carolina	45.4
Arkansas	43.5
South Carolina	40.0
Texas	36.7
Tennessee	33.6
Florida	29.4
Louisiana	24.6

Union South	Percentage
Kentucky	37.9
West Virginia	22.6
Missouri	21.7
District of Columbia	20.6

Others	Percentage
Maine	21.9

B. Combined Baptist and Methodist Proportion of Church Population

Confederate South	Percentage	Percentage Methodist
Georgia	93.2	40.6
Mississippi	90.4	38.2
Alabama	89.6	43.4
South Carolina	89.5	49.5
North Carolina	85.7	40.3
Arkansas	85.1	41.6
Virginia	80.5	27.2

(continued)

TABLE 3.2 (*continued*)

Florida	79.1	49.7
Tennessee	74.0	40.4
Texas	69.0	37.3
Louisiana	41.0	16.4
Union South	*Percentage*	*Percentage Methodist*
West Virginia	67.4	44.8
Kentucky	61.2	23.3
Delaware	57.1	53.0
Missouri	43.8	22.1
District of Columbia	38.0	17.4
Maryland	36.9	32.6
Others	*Percentage*	*Percentage Methodist*
Kansas	38.7	28.5
Maine	36.3	14.4
Indiana	36.0	25.9
Nebraska	29.0	22.1
Washington	28.3	21.6
Iowa	28.1	22.0
Ohio	28.0	22.4

Note: All states are recorded where either Baptists or Methodists numbered at least 20% of a state's church population.

Source: Edwin Scott Gaustad and Philip L. Barlow, *New Historical Atlas of Religion in America* (New York: Oxford University Press, 2001), 376–81, sec. C.17.

was considerable, especially in the South where the white churches played such an important role in overthrowing Reconstruction. For the longer term, however, it was important that a very different story was also under way, since the postbellum configuration of southern religion also provided enough space for independent African-American churches to develop, and they would later play a similarly important part in overthrowing Jim Crow.

National Politics

The combination of religion and race that ended Reconstruction profoundly affected the nation's politics, and for a very long time. The "redemption" of the white South represented, in the first instance, a functional repeal of the Fourteenth and Fifteenth amendments. American citizens were widely and repeatedly denied their rights without due process of law. A large segment of the American citizenry was denied the right to vote. Comprehensive state-by-state comparisons of electoral participation are striking. Throughout the nation in the period from 1870 to 1950, state voter turnout as a percentage of national voter turnout varied for most states within a narrow range. A few states, such as Connecticut, Indiana, Iowa, and New Jersey, regularly witnessed voter turnouts at 120% or so of the national average. Turnouts in a few states like California, Colorado, and California regularly dipped below the national average on the order of 80% to 90%. In the former slave states that did not join the Confederacy, and where black populations represented a smaller percentage than in the former Confederate states (Delaware, Kentucky, Maryland, Missouri, and West Virginia), voting turnout mostly came close to the national average. But in the states of the former Confederacy, where the large black populations were systematically barred from the polls, voter turnout was astonishingly low. In 1880, the year of the last national election with a strong federal presence still active in some of these states, voter turnout in North Carolina, South Carolina, and Florida was actually higher than the national average. By 1920, it had fallen considerably below the national average in Florida, North Carolina, and Tennessee (with turnouts lower than all but one or two of the nonsouthern states). In Alabama,

TABLE 3.3

State Voter Turnout as a Percentage of National Voter Turnout
(fifteen lowest percentages, plus ties)

1860	1880	1900	1920	1940	1960	1980	2000
LA 63	**LA** 30	**MS** 23	**SC** 17	**SC** 16	**MS** 40	DC 67	HI 82
RI 73	RI 61	**SC** 25	**MS** 19	**MS** 24	**AL** 49	**SC** 77	AZ 86
VT 78	**GA** 62	**LA** 29	**GA** 21	**GA** 28	**SC** 49	NV 78	**TX** 87
MA 81	**MS** 63	**GA** 33	**VA** 39	**AR** 29	**GA** 51	**GA** 79	CA 89
TX 83	CO 72	**FL** 41	**AL** 42	**AL** 30	**VA** 54	HI 83	**GA** 89
ME 85	**AL** 74	**AL** 53	**AR** 42	**VA** 35	**AR** 64	AZ 85	NV 89
MO 85	**AR** 75	**AR** 56	**TX** 44	**LA** 47	**TX** 66	**TX** 85	WV 93
NC 87	**VA** 81	WY 70	**LA** 47	**TX** 48	**LA** 70	**NC** 87	**SC** 94
CA 88	CA 85	ME 77	**FL** 62	TN 49	**FL** 78	**VA** 90	NM 96
VA 88	NE 85	RI 77	TN 72	**FL** 65	TN 79	NY 91	AR 97
CT 90	MN 87	TN 77	MA 83	**NC** 68	AZ 84	**FL** 92	**MS** 99
KY 91	**TX** 87	VT 79	PA 87	AZ 91	**NC** 85	**AL** 93	OK 99
MN 92	MA 90	**VA** 81	**NC** 91	MD 92	MD 91	CA 93	DC 100
AL 97	KY 95	**TX** 84	VT 92	KY 95	HI 92	TN 93	IN 100
PA 97	MI 95	OR 80	AZ 95	OK 97	AK 93	KY 95	NY 100
WI 97	TN 95		ME 95			MD 95	**TN** 100

Note: States of the former Confederacy in **bold** type.

Source: Susan B. Carter et al., eds., *Historical Statistics of the United States: Millennial Edition* (New York: Cambridge University Press, 2006). I thank Ethan Sanders for help in preparing this table.

Arkansas, Louisiana, Texas, and Virginia, voter turnout was only one-third to two-fifths the average of the rest of the nation. In Georgia, Mississippi, and South Carolina, it was one-fifth or lower. (See table 3.3.)

In terms of electoral votes, these low turnouts meant that the people who did show up at the polls in those states enjoyed a much greater electoral clout than anywhere else in the nation. Thus, in the presidential contest of 1900 between William Jennings Bryan and William McKinley, each electoral vote in Colorado was the product of over 55,000 popular votes. In seven other states, each electoral vote required at least 40,000 popular votes. But in the former Confederate South, the number of popular votes for each

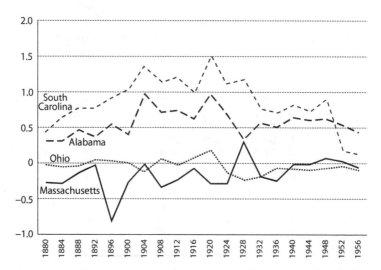

Figure 3.1. State Democratic Vote as Percentage of National Democratic Vote, 1880–1956

electoral vote fell precipitously, in most cases to 16,000 or less, and in Florida, Georgia, Louisiana, Mississippi, and South Carolina to less than 10,000. With blacks systematically excluded and almost all statewide offices decided by results of the state Democratic primaries, the general elections for national office were almost meaningless. Not only had "redemption" violated the Constitution; it also killed democracy.

A second effect of the religiously backed racial end of Reconstruction was to reshape national electoral politics. As figure 3.1 indicates, once the conflicts of Reconstruction were over, the South became a solidly Democratic enclave. Merely by winning the presidential nomination, Democratic candidates were halfway to winning the national election. Conversely, Republican presidential candidates benefited from wariness elsewhere in the country about the southern lock on the Democratic Party.

The retreat from Reconstruction may have been felt even more strongly in political thinking than in electoral results. For both Democrats and Republicans after 1876, the ideology of a regional racist regime profoundly affected national attitudes toward central government power. For eighty-five years after 1876, expansion of central government authority on *any* question was checked by resistance to central government authority on *all* racial questions. The straitjacket placed on national political action by small-government Democrats, often in alliance with small-government Republicans, meant that race continually influenced national political affairs, even on issues where race did not seem involved. As William Jennings Bryan discovered when he proposed more aggressive national policies during his three campaigns for president, a few reforms involving greater federal authority might be implemented, but the barriers protecting southern jurisdiction over southern life were too strong ever to be overcome simply. An example is the political forces at work in the 1890s when Bryan and other populist Democrats proposed public ownership of the railroads as a way of corralling giant corporations and calming labor unrest in the industry. Michael Kazin has noted that southern legislators objected, not primarily for reasons concerning labor and capital, but because "handing that same authority over to Washington bureaucrats threatened the entire tradition of local and state control over racial matters, which many a Dixie lawmaker or his father had taken up arms to preserve."[36] Moreover, national control of the railroads was an unusually sensitive issue in an era when the Supreme Court chose to cement its approval of public-facility segregation in a case of a Louisiana Creole trying to sit in a whites-only railroad compartment (*Plessy v. Ferguson*, 1896).

Only when populist pressure within the South could be harnessed to reforms like the income tax and the popular election of senators, or when evangelical causes, like support for prohibition, gained southern backing, was it possible to give national government broader authority over national life. Otherwise the race-protected facts of regional political hegemony hamstrung efforts at national reform.

The effects of this cramped political position were twofold. First, racist convictions successfully dictated national actions, or the absence of national actions. Second, racist convictions successfully preempted a general debate on whether and how national government power should be used. So long as the racist regimes, buttressed by Jim Crow laws, prevailed, few such debates took place. When in the 1950s and 1960s civil rights reform finally broke through to overthrow these regimes and to restart a national debate on the use of central government authority, the arguments and decisions that resulted continued to bear the impress of the long history of racially mandated national policy.

Observations

The religiously sanctioned racial situation at the end of the nineteenth century, as well as the racially determined political situation, had important consequences for several central aspects of national culture.

The Bible
After the Civil War a decisive shift took place in the relative weight of American social authorities. The Bible might still

be read by millions of citizens to shape their private lives and influence their immediate surroundings. The Bible might also be invoked in the crusade against alcohol—though not read too carefully, since the scriptural teaching in favor of prohibition was even weaker than the nonexistent scriptural testimony in favor of black-only slavery. But the Bible no longer functioned as the nation's preeminent moral authority of choice, as it had functioned so powerfully in the nation's divided mind on slavery through the decades before 1860.

Increasingly after the war, the exalted place that had once been held by Scripture in the national consciousness was replaced by heightened commitments to a national civil religion and to the authority of scientific expertise. As many historians, especially David Blight and Harry Stout, have observed, the bloodletting of the Civil War created a new sense of national destiny, which after the war led to a heightened sense of God's providential design for the whole nation, South and North reunited as one.[37] This flourishing religion of American messianism was still evangelical in its language and ethos, still biblicist in its reservoir of tropes, but ultimate concern had shifted from a transcendent deity to an immanent nation. Both the suspension of concern for black civil rights and the willingness of the nation to embark on imperial adventures were related to the new strength of the nation's civil religion.

Just as strong was the emerging reputation of science. Academic support for evolutionary theory in history, language, archeology, and social developments grew as reliance on precritical interpretations of Scripture declined. As part of this process, more of the nation's reading public displayed a growing willingness to break loose from biblical cosmologies on the subject of race.[38] Increased deference to ethnologists like Josiah Nott, who held that blacks constituted a different species from whites, made it easier to justify treating African Americans as unworthy of full *human* rights.[39] These opinions pushed in the same direction as religious views that invoked Scripture to justify treating blacks as less than fully worthy of God's providential care. (Such biblical conclusions often involved the hypothesis of pre-Adamitism, a theory that treated only Caucasians as the descendents of Adam and Eve and so ended with the same practical disregard of African-American civil rights as polygenetic theories favored by secularists.)[40]

In the postbellum decades, as American respect for science grew rapidly, scientific reasons for discounting the humanity of African Americans came to exercise a greater influence than religious reasons. The prevalence of lynching, which grew in frequency and ferocity toward the end of the nineteenth century, reflected the effects of scientifically sanctioned views of black inferiority, as well as the continuation of religiously inspired white opinion.

The shifting fortunes of Scripture in American public life can be summarized like this: During the antebellum period, the supreme authority of the Bible was used to justify slavery and also, in many minds, black-only slavery, though there also existed some use of the Bible to defend treatment of slaves as full human beings and some use to argue against any slavery reserved for blacks only. In postbellum decades, the authority of national civil religion and of scientific expertise was used to rationalize treatment of African Americans as subcitizens and subhumans, though there also existed some use of the Bible to defend African Americans as full human beings and some use to defend full civil rights for blacks. Before the war, the confusion of slavery and race compromised the authority of the Bible; after the war, the acceptance of science and national civil religion as ultimate authorities relativized the authority of the Bible.[41]

The Courts

As standard histories now make clear, the U.S. judiciary offered only a little resistance to the white supremacist convictions that came to prevail by the end of the nineteenth century.[42] Because of how southern "redemption" and the reconciliation of Union and Confederate came to define national values in general, jurisprudence followed local social mores, free-market reasoning, civil religion, and the wisdom of scientific experts—but not the Bible or the original intent of the Thirteenth, Fourteenth, and Fifteenth amendments—in important decisions on race from the mid-1870s onward.

In parallel to congressional retreat from Reconstruction, the courts proved unwilling to enforce the claims of citizenship stipulated in the Civil War amendments. Congress had passed Enforcement Acts in 1870 and 1871, which were designed to restrain the Ku Klux Klan and other white supremacist groups from choking off African-American voting. An additional Civil Rights Act of 1875 prohibited racial discrimination in all public accommodations. But already in 1873 the Supreme Court ruled in *The Slaughter House Cases* that the "privileges or immunities" guaranteed to all citizens by the Fourteenth Amendment had to be construed very narrowly.[43] Then in 1876 the justices held in *United States v. Rees et al.* and *United States v. Cruikshank* that voting was a matter for state supervision.[44] In 1883 the Court ruled that the Civil Rights Act of 1875 was unconstitutional because it prohibited racial discrimination by private persons, rather than just by states, in providing public services. This ruling again focused on the letter of the Fourteenth Amendment ("No state shall make or enforce any law which shall abridge the privileges or immunities of citizens of the United States").[45] By so doing it completed the evisceration of what the amendment's drafters and ratifiers had intended to accomplish.

When in 1896 the Supreme Court ruled that Louisiana's segregation of rail car accommodations was constitutional, Justice John Harlan's famous dissent in *Plessy v. Ferguson* stated clearly how much this decision abrogated the Civil War amendments to the Constitution: "The sure guaranty of the peace and security of each race is the clear, distinct, unconditional recognition by our governments, national and state, of every right that inheres in civil freedom, and of the equality before the law of all citizens of the United States, without regard to race." The accuracy of his prediction, that this decision would one day be considered an evil on a par with the *Dred Scott* decision of 1857 that denied any black the status of citizen, was matched by the accuracy of what he predicted for conditions between the races so long as legislation like Louisiana's was upheld: "State enactments regulating the enjoyment of civil rights upon the basis of race, and cunningly devised to defeat legitimate results of the war . . . can have no other result than to render permanent peace impossible, and to keep alive a conflict of races, the continuance of which must do harm to all concerned."[46]

Yet at the time there was scant attention to what Harlan was predicting for the future. Racial discrimination had become a nearly settled fact, and the court majority rather than the Harlan dissent reflected the general will of the nation. The case of *Giles v. Harris* from 1903, where an African American from Alabama sued to overturn state practices that had the effect of restricting voter registration to whites, revealed the entrenchment of settled opinion. In this case there were significant dissenters, including Justice David Brewer, who thought that the plaintiff had made his case: "He alleges that he is a citizen of Alabama, entitled to vote; that he desired to vote at an election for representative in Congress; that without registration he could not vote, and that registration was wrongfully denied him by the defendants." But Oliver Wendell Holmes, ruling for the majority, held differently. Holmes acknowledged that Alabama law, which limited voting to "all persons who are of good character and who understand the duties and obligations of citizenship under a republican form of government," was being used by county registrars to exclude almost all black people from voting. But then, in effect, he threw up his hands and conceded that conditions were far stronger than the law: it was "impossible to grant the equitable relief which was asked" because "the traditional limits of proceedings in equity have not embraced a remedy for political wrongs."[47] As such rulings implied, the Supreme Court was willing to use a great deal of conventional wisdom—reflecting religious opinion, popular instinct, ethnographic science, and societal mores—in coming to its decisions. By 1923, in the case of *United States v. Bhagat Singh Thind*, government lawyers mixed consideration of "race," "religion," and "civilization" to convince the court that a high-caste Indian Hindu—that is, a Caucasian—could not be considered "white" under U.S. law, and so could be stripped of his citizenship.[48]

The judicial record coming out of the Reconstruction period did not represent a mindless conformity to social prejudice, for rulings were carefully drafted and were always based on valid points of law or procedure. Yet in their manifest insistence on privileging discrimination in the states (no matter how substantively that discrimination violated the intentions of the Civil War amendments) and in their manifest reliance on the ideological spirit of the age (where scientific expertise and popular social prejudice were becoming more important than values of human universality backed by either theology or secular reason), the courts were only enforcing the racist regime that, in the wake of southern "redemption," held sway in the nation.

Long-term Effects

The religious-racial-political effects of the Civil War were extremely far-reaching. It was especially important that central government authority succeeded in reuniting the country and in making slavery illegal but failed to dislodge systemic racial discrimination. Yet it is also necessary to be realistic about what was actually possible at the time, especially from the perspective of the early twenty-first century when living memory is fading rapidly about how strongly the nineteenth-century racist assumptions prevailed in all segments of white society, religious and nonreligious, highly educated and illiterate, northern as well as southern. Only a massive federal presence maintained vigilantly for thirty, forty, or even fifty years might have rooted black political participation and black legal equality deeply enough to withstand the tempests of reaction and swelling undercurrents of indifference. In the event, the tempests, which were very strong in the South and also in a few areas elsewhere, and the undercurrents, which were strong in every region of the country, won out over central government action. Thereafter, central government inaction facilitated the process by which racial discrimination and racial prejudice, even in the absence of slavery, worsened from the 1870s for more than the next half-century.

The failure of the central government to move effectively against racial discrimination was not exactly *caused* by the failures of evangelical religion during and after the Civil War. But the acceptance by evangelicals, who had done so much to shape the nation in so many other ways, of a racist regime after the war was everywhere a contextual factor in the weakening of central government action during Reconstruction and its caving in to the "redemption" of a white racist South. This same acceptance was also an important factor in the retreat of the main white denominations from advocacy on behalf of African Americans. What was true for white evangelicals about sanctioning a racist America was for the most part just as true for other Protestants and Roman Catholics.

Nonetheless and critically, after the social hegemony of white evangelical Protestants gave way, it helped create enough free space for a distinctly African-American form of experiential, quasi-evangelical, universal, and reforming Christianity to get up from its bed and start to walk. That miracle, however underestimated at the time, would one day bring about a fundamental alteration in the shape of American political life.

CHAPTER IV

Religion and the Civil Rights Movement

The controversies that brought on the Civil War, along with the consequences of the war as resolved (or unresolved) in Reconstruction, set the course of national politics into the 1960s. Throughout, race in conjunction with religion was of first importance. Before and during the Civil War, religiously motivated people heightened the political antithesis over slavery even as they shied away from confronting issues of race. After the Civil War, religion receded before other influences as the determining force in national political life, even as it retained great strength for individuals and communities in several variations and in many regions of the country. Yet while it was thinning as a proactive political force, religion remained powerful on many other levels— for example, by helping to subvert Reconstruction and the possibility of a racially just society, and by doing so much to make African-American self-determination possible.

In the decades between the reimposition of southern white rule and the end of World War II, religion exerted only a sporadic influence on national politics. While race remained a prime determinant of American political life, no significant religious stimuli raised the salience of race as earlier biblical convictions had amplified antebellum arguments over slavery and as white Christian actions (and inaction) had hastened the end of Reconstruction. These intervening decades represented a lull before once again the civil rights movement, along with cultural and political movements inspired by the mobilization for civil rights, reignited the race-religion dynamic as a critical factor in political history.

To be sure, religion did surface episodically in the intervening years as a political force. The temperance crusade that led to the Eighteenth Amendment in 1919 represented a last gasp of the "evangelical united front" of the nineteenth century, which, except on temperance, was busily dividing itself into mutually antagonistic submovements.[1] Fundamentalist-modernist controversy, the rise of Pentecostalism, the growing strength of ethnic Protestant churches, and—above all—the emergence of the Catholic church as a national force, all contributed to a fragmentation of religious energy in American political life. The fact that prohibition was only a modest social success and that it could not sustain widespread popular support indicated the relative marginality of the religious forces that inspired the temperance movement.

The 1928 presidential election also showed that ancient Protestant-Catholic antagonisms were still capable of exerting a political impact. As the graph of state-by-state voting suggests (see fig. 3.1 above), in 1928 Democratic support for the Catholic Al Smith dipped dramatically in the strongly evangelical South, while it rose dramatically in several other strongly Catholic states, especially Rhode Island and Massachusetts.

By comparison with 1924, the ratio of state Democratic support to national Democratic support dropped sharply in overwhelmingly Protestant states, especially where the Protestant majority was strongly Baptist (e.g., Alabama, 1.60 to 1.26; Arkansas, 1.56 to 1.03; Florida, 1.43 to 0.98; Georgia, 1.80 to 1.37; Kentucky, 1.12 to 0.99; Texas, 1.76 to 1.18).[2] The reverse was true in several states with strong Catholic populations (e.g., Illinois 0.90 to 1.04, Louisiana 1.68 to 1.87, Massachusetts 0.82 to 1.23, Rhode Island 0.88 to 1.23). Yet after that one election, national voting mostly returned to patterns that had been set in the immediate wake of Reconstruction and that would remain in place for the next quarter century. When in 1960 another Catholic Democrat, John F. Kennedy, was nominated for president, there was another Protestant-Catholic reaction, with a strengthening of the Democratic vote among Catholics and a strengthened Republican vote among Protestants. But the reaction in this election was not as important as the broader realignment then underway in the 1960s as a result of the civil rights revolution. (See fig. 5.1, p. 154.)

The one great exception to the historical American pattern of political change being driven by religion and race was electoral response to the Great Depression. The rise of the Democratic Party to national dominance, the creation of the New Deal coalition, and the general expansion of government action in response to economic crisis brought significant and enduring political change that was not primarily caused by the forces of race and religion. The shift of African-American voters from the Republican Party to the Democrats was one of the most long-lasting electoral results of the Depression era. Black voters knew that President Roosevelt was not particularly active on civil rights, but a large majority concluded that his economic policies were exactly what they needed. African-American praise for Roosevelt could employ a strongly religious vocabulary, as when he was hailed as "America's salvation" and "a God-sent man." But the shift to FDR and the Democrats represented, in Nancy Weiss's judicious phrase, "a pragmatic political response" rather than anything religiously motivated.[3] As the figures suggest, however, even when the New Deal changed much, it did not change the relative political alignment of states and regions that had been solidified in the wake of Reconstruction.

After World War II, American politics reprised the earlier, more enduring pattern with deep-seated changes driven by race in consort with religion. Thus, political history since the 1950s, with deep crosscurrents between religion and politics, represents both discontinuity with the recent past (the New Deal) and continuity with American history more generally. The continuity was supplied by conditions defined by race that, with full involvement of the churches, were fixed in place from the 1850s to the 1880s and remained substantially unchanged for the next three-quarters of a century.

The story of the recent past is complex in the extreme, but for my purposes it can be summarized in a sequence of three major developments. First, the civil rights movement fundamentally altered the course of U.S. political history. That movement was driven by a number of important influences, but the impetus provided by black religion was critical for its emergence and also its success. When the spark of African-American faith, which had been hidden under a bushel, finally burned bright in the nation, America was changed. Second, the civil rights movement gained a measure of success for a number of reasons, but arguably the most important is that religious support for it was unusually strong while religious opposition to it was relatively weak. Third, the civil rights movement precipitated a thorough realignment in national political power and a dramatic alteration in the nation's public ethos. The realignment took place when voting was reconfigured in support of civil rights reforms or in reactions against forces associated with those reforms. That reaction was motivated in part by racist impulses, but also by broader resentment at the expansion of central government authority exercised in the federal enforcement of civil rights. The alteration in ethos took place when other groups followed the path of civil rights activists and began to use religious or quasi-religious rhetoric in support of their political goals.

Since the 1950s, change in American politics has been driven by a bewildering welter of social, demographic, media, foreign policy, and economic forces. Yet directly related to many of these forces, and indirectly connected to all, has been the nexus of race and religion. This chapter and the next are admittedly skewed, since they highlight religious factors at the expense of other important influences. But by focusing in this chapter on the religious origins of the civil rights movement and in the next on connections between civil rights and the broader course of recent political history, my admittedly partial account should indicate how the nation's recent political history has testified to the intimate but tangled relations of race and religion.

African-American Religion before the Civil Rights Movement

African-American religion, particularly as it had been developing from the end of slavery, provided the indispensable foundation for the civil rights movement. To be sure, much else besides black religion fed into the movement, including local community organizing, legal challenges to segregation and racially based voting restrictions, consciousness-raising in the North as well as the South by white religious leaders, strenuous advocacy grounded in secular motives, and much more. But the conviction, as summarized by David Chappell, that "God was on their side" was foundational in driving the advocates of civil rights and sustaining them until at least some of their goals were met.[4]

Three points are important for clarifying the African-American religion that has meant so much for contemporary history. First, the intellectually sophisticated convictions of educated movement leaders like Martin Luther King, Jr., represented a compound of many elements. Second, the sophisticated convictions of such leaders were matched and balanced by the precritical beliefs of many civil rights foot soldiers whose religion remained close to the elemental faiths of the nineteenth century. Third, the particular history of African-American thought explains why the faith that drove the civil rights movement differed markedly from other varieties of American religion.

The Faith of Leaders

The religion that inspired the civil rights movement was a complex amalgamation in which the justly lionized contributions of Martin Luther King, Jr., and other visible leaders represented only one element.[5] This elite element, as even casual observers know, was powerful. It is sometimes not realized, however, how variegated it was. Historically considered, it grew from a root of prophetic evangelical biblicism stretching back through Henry McNeal Turner and Elias Camp Morris to Daniel Alexander Payne and beyond.

The religion of King and his associates was always more than just black evangelical revivalism, but it was never less.

Yet the root of <u>prophetic biblicism</u> had also been watered by several other important influences, some of which came from whites. In King's case the Social Gospel teachings of Walter Rauschenbusch, which he learned at Rochester Theological Seminary (Rauschenbusch's old institution) from Professor George W. Davis, outlined one way to turn classical Christian beliefs from otherworldly to social purposes.[6] In his doctoral studies at Boston University, King also absorbed elements from the philosophical personalism taught by Edgar S. Brightman. This perspective contended for a heightened philosophical evaluation of human free will along with a stronger sense of God as bounded by the actions of the humans he had created.[7] The postliberal Christian realism of Reinhold Niebuhr was even more important for King and some of his associates, primarily for what it affirmed about the intractability of human evil alongside the possibilities of human morality. More specifically, Niebuhr as early as the late 1920s was writing about the <u>deep injustices inflicted on American blacks</u>; soon thereafter he was promoting <u>non-violent tactics as potentially powerful tools</u> in working for social justice.[8] In both emphases, he was opening a door through which some black leaders were eager to pass.

On nonviolence, which became the key theoretical and crucial practical engine of civil rights agitation, the movement also absorbed several influences even more important than Niebuhr's. When A. J. Muste, longtime head of the Fellowship of Reconciliation, died in early 1967, King said that without his contribution, "the American Negro might never have caught the meaning of nonviolence."[9] Muste experienced a conversion in the mid-1930s from

Marxist-Leninism to Christian pacifism, after which he taught principles of nonviolent social action to numerous reformers, including the founders of the Congress of Racial Equality. With his own brand of Quaker-influenced pacifism, Muste was also a mentor to some of the most effective teachers of nonviolence, including Bayard Rustin, and he enjoyed personal connections with King from the mid-1950s. Nonviolence also came to King and other movement leaders from the life and teaching of Mahatma Gandhi, although Gandhi's influence on the civil rights movement was mostly mediated through African-American teachers.

Such teachers, who constituted a full generation of creative and insightful intellectuals, were, in fact, the most significant influences for the movement's most visible leaders. From the 1910s to the 1940s, these intellectuals expanded the legacy of nineteenth-century black religious thought into a distinctive form of dynamic Christian witness.

As a few perceptive historians have shown, black religious thought in the interwar years was aggressively on the move.[10] The roster of key individuals included several whose writings and face-to-face teaching played a direct role in the later civil rights movement—King, for example, was a student of Benjamin Mays and George D. Kelsey at Morehouse College. But perhaps even more important than specific contributions by individuals was the creation of an entire body of thought, arising out of the historic black churches, but fructified by fresh injections from a wide range of world sources ranging from the pacifism of Mahatma Gandhi to the socialism of labor organizer A. Philip Randolph.

Moredecai W. Johnson, as the longtime president of Howard University, encouraged many of these thinkers to push religious analysis out of narrow ecclesiastical channels into broader engagement with society.[11] Benjamin Mays, the dean of the Howard Divinity School and then from 1946 the president of Morehouse College, early on outlined much that would be developed more fully by others in his train. His 1933 volume, *The Negro's Church*, authored with Joseph W. Nicholson, a minister of the Colored Methodist Episcopal Church, used an extensive survey of black rural and urban congregations to demonstrate that African-American congregations responded very positively to messages stressing the brotherhood of all races. The authors catalogued many shortcomings of education, perspective, and social condition, but they could also affirm that "the Negro church generally preaches love and tolerance toward all races and abides by these ideals in practice."[12]

Nicholson would go on to be one of the most important church leaders supporting the organizing efforts of Randolph and other labor leaders. For his part, Mays in 1938 published a much-noticed book, *The Negro's God, as Reflected in His Literature*, and in 1939 a little-noticed pamphlet, "The American Negro and the Christian Religion." These works advanced a picture of Jesus as a model of servanthood, taught the brotherhood of all humanity, and spoke of racial pride as a sin.

The war years, when A. Philip Randolph and other black leaders challenged the national government to show the same commitment to freedom for African Americans it was working to deliver for the subjugated people of Europe and Asia, also stimulated religious leaders to deeper considerations of the social implications of Christian faith. Randolph's advocacy was especially important. He was the son of an AME minister, socialist candidate for public office, and leader of the Brotherhood of Sleeping Car Porters, and his success in working for the desegregation of labor unions and then the military—as well as his ability to coordinate the efforts of different civil rights groups—offered practical guidelines for pushing toward other social reforms. Randolph himself often showed the way, as he would do in August 1963 by chairing the historic March for Jobs and Freedom in Washington, D.C.

In 1945 the Baptist Richard I. McKinney, president of Storer College in West Virginia, published with Yale University Press a book, *Religion in Higher Education among Negroes*, that expanded on the theme of Christian brotherhood as the key element in religious higher education. The study was also significant for how it balanced a positive assessment of potential religious contributions from African-American institutions with a realistic account of contextual realities: "Because of the caste society in which Negroes live, there are fundamental psychological, social, and spiritual problems which the youth of this minority face. The religious program of the college has an indispensable role to play in the solution of the problems of personality adjustment which are engendered by a caste society."[13]

The influence of Gandhi came, in large measure, from Howard Thurman, who was dean of the chapel at Howard Divinity School from 1932 to 1944 before he took other positions in San Francisco and Boston. His book published in 1949, *Jesus and the Disinherited* featured a retelling of his five-hour response to a challenge from a Hindu in Gandhi's circle when Thurman was on a trip to India. He reported the challenge like this:

> You have lived in a Christian nation in which you are segregated, lynched, and burned. Even in the church, I understand, there is segregation. . . . I am a Hindu. I do not understand. Here you are in my country,

standing deep within the Christian faith and tradition. I do not wish to seem rude to you. But, sir, I think you are a traitor to all the darker peoples of the earth. I am wondering what you, an intelligent man, can say in defense of your position.[14]

Thurman's reply described a Jesus who was poor, outcast, and despised by the elites of his world, but in whom all the poor, outcast, and despised of the world could hope. Those who read Thurman in the 1940s found him promoting belief in "the literal truth of God," but also exploring the religious implications of social, economic, and political conditions.

Shortly before Thurman published his account of this dialogue, William Stuart Nelson, a professor at Howard, brought out an edited volume, *The Christian Way in Race Relations*, in which he also made extensive use of insights acquired during trips to India and the Far East. From Gandhi, Nelson took a definition of religion as summarized by love of the other, and a definition of sin that included economic injustice. To Nelson, when Jesus accepted the cross, he was demonstrating the extraordinary power of pacifism put to the use of human brotherhood.

The importance of black religious thought from the 1930s and 1940s for what came later in the 1950s and 1960s can be illustrated by the arguments, the perspectives, and even the form of words found in Nelson's colloquium. In this volume, which was almost as full of challenge for blacks to act with Christian integrity as of admonition for American society to end its sinful oppression of blacks, a number of authors enunciated themes that would become the public mainstay of the later civil rights movement. Nelson, as editor, articulated a rationale for the book by pointing out how rich were the African-American resources—"There is the church, there are the Christian associations, Christian colleges, certain nonecclesiastical organizations, and there are individuals"—for showing "the practicability of Christianity in relation to social problems."[15] Benjamin Mays, in describing "The Obligations of Individual Christians," combined imperatives for courageous honesty in addressing the reality of racial discrimination with equally strong injunctions for maintaining Christian principles of love in all struggles for civil rights: "Despite jim crow, segregation, and discrimination, which he meets almost incessantly, the Negro Christian does not have to hate white people. Even when he piles up evidence to prove that efforts are being made to keep him a second-class citizen, it is not foreordained of God that he has to nurture rancor in his heart and hate in his soul."[16]

In an essay with particularly strong anticipation of many prominent themes of the later civil rights movement, Mays's colleague at Morehouse, George Kelsey, defined "The Christian Way in Race Relations." To Kelsey the Christian doctrines of God as Creator, God as Judge, and God as Redeemer spelled out a thorough religious individualism (persons in relation to God) alongside a thorough religious universalism (all of the human race in relation to God). The individualism led to hope for the future, but tinctured with the need for rigorous self-criticism and self-restraint. The universalism led to belief in the coming Kingdom of God, but expressed with realism about the difficulties of moving now toward the universal values of that kingdom. Kelsey's powerful conclusion addressed, as would Martin Luther King, Jr.'s famous *Letter from Birmingham City Jail* (1963), those who counseled caution on civil rights because "the time is not ripe." To Kelsey, such counsel was "a stench in the nostrils of God." He also referred "to the need of prophecy"—for, that is, leaders who would dare to proclaim "thus saith the Lord" and so "make hearts burn" in attacking "the problem of caste in America." And in phrases that would be echoed by King's best-known speech at the March on Washington sixteen years later in August 1963, Kelsey's very last word was that God's "prophets must speak and they must be prepared to be stoned, for Jerusalem always stones her prophets. But at length the people will hear the voice of God saying, 'Let judgment roll down as waters, and righteousness as a mighty stream.'"[17]

The elite thought contributed by figures like Mays, Nicholson, McKinney, Kelsey, and Thurman has never received its due, in part because it was given scant attention by the broader world when their major works were published, in part because the later development of the civil rights movement lost at least some awareness of its strongly theological roots. It was, nonetheless, a powerful message these figures were working up, especially by joining classical Christian themes to principles of nonviolence. Historically considered, it paralleled in its influence what active Methodist, Baptist, and Presbyterian preachers of the early nineteenth century had accomplished in the nation's highways and byways as they proclaimed the themes that shaped the national culture of that era.

The Faith of Followers

Formal religious thought from elites was always complemented in the civil rights movement by a less cerebral, more visceral version of the Christian faith that remained closer to the ardent supernaturalism and straightforward biblicism of the autonomous black denominations and, beyond them, of slave religion. The second important point about the

African-American religion that drove the civil rights movement is that it included much faith that knew not Gandhi or Philip Randolph, but that had gone deep into the lives of countless ordinary believers. David Chappell has persuasively argued that this faith—with its "fundamentalist" experience of miracles and dramatic conversions—made an essential contribution in transforming the theoretical imperative of civil rights reform into a prophetic power able to move events.[18]

To be sure, this faith had been severely censured by W.E.B. DuBois and other frustrated reformers who castigated its adherents as drugged by an opiate that disabled them from effective action in the here and now. But Charles Payne, who has written perceptively about the life-and-death struggles of the civil rights movement in Mississippi, understood things better when he described the strongly supernaturalist and otherwordly faith practiced in tight black community churches, usually with females predominating: "A more flexible model [than thinking of this religion as an opiate] might hold that involvement in such commitments ordinarily militates against involvement in social movements, but once any one person in the network becomes politically involved, the strength of the social ties within the network is likely to draw other members in."[19]

Payne's own research substantiated his theoretical analysis when he followed the civil rights activities of those who read the Bible simplistically, looked for immediate consolation from an active God, and held precritical views of Jesus Christ and the Holy Spirit as acting directly in the everyday world for redemptive purposes. He found that such ones, once they had been galvanized into social action, were able to exert the same force in the public sphere as they had experienced in their private religious lives. There was, for example, Lou Emma Allen, who after a lifetime of mistreatment at the hands of Mississippi whites, could say, "Of course, there is no way I can hate anybody and hope to see God's face." There was also Annell Ponder, who was jailed in Winona, Mississippi, with other black reformers and then beaten by guards when she refused to address them as "sir." As reported by a friend who was waiting for her own attention from the guards, "But anyway, she kept screamin', and they kept beating on her, and finally she started prayin' for 'em, and she asked God to have mercy on 'em, because they didn't know what they was doin'."[20]

The friend was Mrs. Fannie Lou Hamer, whose experiences in the Winona jail are at the center of Charles Marsh's book, *God's Long Summer*, and whose leadership in 1964 of Mississippi's Freedom Democratic Party has been well chronicled.[21] After she was beaten in the Winona jail, she had a chance to speak with the jailer's wife and daughter, who brought water and ice to the prisoners:

> And I told them, "Y'all is nice. You must be Christian people." The jailer's wife told me she tried to live a Christian life. And I told her I would like her to read two scriptures in the Bible, and I tol' her to read the 26th Chapter of Proverbs and the 26th Verse ["Whose hatred is covered by deceit, his wickedness shall be showed before the whole congregation"]. She taken it down on a paper. And then I told her to read the [17th] Chapter of Acts and the 26th Verse ["Hath made of one blood all nations of men for to dwell on all the face of the earth"]. And she taken that down. And she never did come back after then.[22]

As many of the histories of the Civil Rights Movement have documented, reform was born aloft on the wings of song, preeminently black gospel and classical evangelical hymnody. When in 1965 King and his associates in the Southern Christian Leadership Conference were discussing where in the North they should take the civil rights campaign, one midsized city was ruled out because it could not assemble an adequate choir.[23] Most famously, the signature anthem of the movement, "We Shall Overcome," bespoke a history from deep within the tradition of black plebeian faith. In 1916 Charles A. Tindley, the pioneer of professional gospel music, included in his hymnal *New Songs of Praise* a song called "I'll Overcome Some Day":

> Both seen and unseen powers join
> To drive my soul astray,
> But with His Word a sword of mine,
> I'll overcome some day.
> I'll overcome some day.
> I'll overcome some day. . . .
> Tho' many a time no signs appear
> Of answer when I pray,
> My Jesus says I need not fear,
> He'll make it plain some day.
> I'll be like Him some day.
> I'll be like Him some day.

When this composition was amalgamated with the spiritual "I'll Be All Right" and then sung to the tune of that spiritual, the result was "We Shall Overcome."[24]

One of the great presidential speeches in all of American history was President Lyndon Johnson's address to Congress and the nation on March 15, 1965, in the immediate wake of the violent outrage in Selma, Alabama, when state troopers and a large deputized mob attacked mostly local blacks who were demonstrating peacefully for the right to

register to vote. When Johnson closed his memorable address setting forth the compelling need for a voting rights
bill by intoning "and-we-shall-overcome," he probably did
not realize the depth of African-American history he was
invoking. But along with much else, he was testifying to
the power of one strand in American religion that, however
much it had looked like an opiate, was now revealed as an
elixir of superlative power.

It was similar with the Bible.[25] Some movement leaders
had learned the more enlightened and academically conventional views of biblical higher criticism. But they preached
as if the Book was true in starkly realistic terms. The public
pronouncements, and not just the sermons, from all movement leaders were thick with biblical quotation and allusion.
In that usage, leaders and followers were, literally, on the
same page. The Rev. H. C. Boyd of Shiloh Baptist Church
in Albany, Mississippi, was won over to support the Mississippi Freedom Riders, much against his better judgment,
during the summer of 1961 only because Charles Sherrod
of the Student Nonviolent Coordinating Committee con-
vinced him by quoting chapter and verse from the Scriptures about brotherhood and justice. Later, after Albany's
black community was shaken when Sherrod and other demonstrators were arrested and some of them beaten, a layman calmed the very nervous crowd by leading in prayer
and offering a spontaneous recitation of the Twenty-Third
Psalm.[26] Such moments were repeated constantly in almost
every phase of the southern movement, and also when King
and his associates took the movement into the North.

The fabric of the civil rights movement was woven by
the black churches, which had been knit together in vital
denominations during the years immediately after the Civil
War. Taylor Branch's splendid three volumes on "America

in the King Years" offers grist for a modern Walt Whitman to memorialize these churches and their faithful members. Branch provides a seemingly endless roll call of such African-American congregations—a few well-to-do and dignified, many of humble estate—that volunteered space for meetings, housed out-of-town reformers, mobilized congregations for meals and other support, occasionally served as makeshift hospitals, and provided in general the indispensable infrastructure of the movement. Their names speak simply, but powerfully, of generations nurtured in the consolations and encouragements of the gospel.[27] A partial list includes:

AME Zion Hall (Selma, Ala.)

Antioch Church (Camden County, Ala.)

Bell Flower Baptist (Grenada, Miss.)

Bethel Baptist (Birmingham, Ala.)

Bethlehem Christian Church (Fort Deposit, Ala.)

Bibleway Church (Washington, D.C.)

Brown Chapel AME (Selma, Ala.)

City of St. Jude (Montgomery, Ala.)

Dexter Avenue Baptist (Montgomery, Ala.)

Ebenezer Baptist (Atlanta, Ga.)

First Baptist (Hayneville, Ala.; Nashville, Tenn.; Selma, Ala.; St. Augustine, Fla.)

First Union Baptist (Meridian, Miss.)

Friendship Baptist (Americus, Ga.; Hayneville, Ala.; Greenwood, Miss.)

Green Street Baptist (Selma, Ala.)

Hutchinson St. Baptist (Montgomery, Ala.)

I Hope Baptist (Terrell County, Miss.)

Lawson Centenary Methodist (Memphis, Tenn.)

Liberty Baptist (Chicago, Ill.)

Little Union Baptist (Shreveport, La.)

Maryland Baptist Center (Baltimore, Md.)

Mount Carmel Baptist (Lowndes County, Ala.)

Mount Gillard Missionary Baptist (Lowndes County, Ala.)

Mount Moriah Baptist (Hayneville, Ala.)

Mount Olive Baptist (Terrell County, Miss.)

Mount Zion AME (Longdale, Miss.)

Mount Zion Baptist (Neshoba County, Miss.)

Mount Zion Hill Baptist (McComb, Miss.)

New Friendship Baptist (Chicago, Ill.)

New Hope Missionary Baptist (Grenada, Miss.)

Pearl Street AME (Birmingham, Ala.)

St. James Baptist (Birmingham, Ala.)

St. James CME (Hattiesburg, Miss.)

St. John Methodist (Palmer's Crossing, Miss.)

St. John's United Methodist (Hattiesburg, Miss.)

St. Mary's Baptist (St. Augustine, Fla.)

Saint Paul CME (Savannah, Ga.)

Saint Paul's (Laurel, Miss.)

St. Paul's AME (St. Augustine, Fla.)

St. Paul's Colored Methodist Episcopal (Selma, Ala.)

Shady Grove Baptist (Lee County, Miss.)

Sixteenth St. Baptist (Birmingham, Ala.)

Tabernacle Baptist (Selma, Ala.)

Thurgood Church (Birmingham, Ala.)

Turner Chapel AME (Greenwood, Miss.)

Union Temple Baptist (Atlantic City, N.J.)

Warren Avenue Congregational (Chicago, Ill.)

Wesley Chapel (Greenwood, Miss.)

Williams Chapel Baptist (Ruleville, Miss.)

Zion's Chapel Methodist (Selma, Ala.)

These houses of God were an offering from humble believers that gave notable leaders like Martin Luther King, Jr., the pulpit from which they transfixed the nation.

The particular force of African-American religion in the civil rights movement was its potent mix of more formal elements, which could draw on Gandhi, twentieth-century socialism, and a measure of modern Protestant theology to fill out the raw biblicism of traditional black religion, and all expressed with an array of time-honored customary practices and beliefs. The received religion of the black churches, which had been so invisible for so long, was now being revealed as an explosive public force.

A Distinctive Faith

The third important point to note about this African-American faith is its difference from other traditions of American religion. Both formal and populist strands were rooted in the evangelical Protestantism that African Americans had taken for themselves in the early and mid-nineteenth century. But they were also products of a significant period of independent evolution isolated from genetically similar strands of white evangelicalism. That independent evolutionary development, in turn, brought several adaptations that were critical for the survival of the species of African-American religion.

In particular, several traits that black American Christians displayed by the mid-twentieth century were greatly at odds with some that had become prominent in the evolution of white evangelical religion. These traits included a capacity for cooperation between theological liberals (who tended to picture the work of God in mythic terms) and theological conservatives (who saw the work of God in intensely realistic terms) for the purpose of advancing social goals. After the fundamentalist-modernist controversies, such cooperation all but vanished in the precincts of white Christianity. The thinking that infused the civil rights movement also co-opted ideological elements for religious and social purposes with a flexibility unprecedented in American religious history. During a period when only exotic margins of white Christianity had any interest in the Hindu pacifism of Gandhi or the democratic socialism of A. Philip Randolph, these and other disparate teachings were easily folded into the generally Christian framework of civil rights reform. In addition, the religion of the civil rights movement displayed a capacity that had been mostly absent among whites—especially after William Jennings Bryan passed from the

scene—of organically linking traditional conservative theology and progressive social action. For practical purposes,
that capacity imparted a force that neither the otherworld-
liness of conservative religion nor the aversion to supernaturalism of political liberalism could touch.

In sum, the African-American religion that propelled
the civil rights movement was an American Protestant faith
strongly rooted in the activistic religion of nineteenth-
century revivalistic evangelicalism, but by the 1950s now
quite removed from the faith of white conservatives that
was also strongly rooted in the same religious sources. But,
of course, as a complex phenomenon, much more was involved in civil rights reform than the religion of the reformers themselves.

Broader Contexts

The progress of the civil rights movement of the 1950s and
1960s cannot be explained simply. Its success depended on
a number of contextual factors, some more obviously religious than others. A brief accounting of some of these other
factors will offer a little balance to the picture offered here.
Paying attention to these factors also prepares the way for
understanding how the civil rights movement could spark
the many other social and political changes that are the
subject of chapter 5.

The most important background reality was the expansion
of the federal government. This expansion was pioneered at
the start of the twentieth century by progressives like Teddy
Roosevelt and William Jennings Bryan. It was furthered by
Franklin Roosevelt in the New Deal, strengthened during World War II, and expanded once again in the Great

Society (and Vietnam War) of Lyndon Johnson. From early in the Great Depression of the 1930s and continuing to the present, the focal point of government—whether positive law, judicial action, or bureaucratic function—has been shifting from localities to the nation. Not until 1913 and the passage of the Sixteenth Amendment to the Constitution did the national government enjoy the right to tax American individuals directly, without regard to the apportionment of population by state. Not until Franklin Roosevelt's New Deal policies of the 1930s did national legislation—for banking, old-age pensions, investment, employment relief, and many other matters—begin to be felt directly by individuals. Not until the massive mobilization of World War II did the expenditures and financial policies of the federal government become the dominating center of the American economy. Not until the Soviet launch of the first Sputnik space satellite in 1957 did the federal government begin to fund, encourage, and regulate teaching and learning in the nation's countless public schools. The movement from limited to expanded federal government was a necessary precondition for the implementation of civil rights reform.

Modern judicial history has moved in the same direction, with national solutions increasingly mandated for more and more local problems.[28] An example is provided by alterations in how the separation of church and state was defined, and then adjudicated. On this issue, the first important move came only in 1940 with the application of the Fourteenth Amendment to the religious provisions of the First Amendment. The Fourteenth Amendment had been aimed expressly at the states, which were prohibited from making or enforcing "any law which shall abridge the privileges or immunities of citizens of the United States," and had further restrained states from denying any of their citizens "life, liberty, or property, without due process of law." In 1940 the U.S. Supreme Court ruled (*Cantwell v. Connecticut*) that by the application of this Fourteenth Amendment, the First Amendment's prohibition of a religious establishment and its guarantee of religious "free exercise" must apply to state laws as well.[29]

The second key ruling came in 1947 with a case concerning a New Jersey law providing bus transportation for students in private, religious schools as well as for students in public schools (*Everson v. Board of Education*). Although the Supreme Court upheld the law, it also made an extreme claim about the implications of the First Amendment. In a judgment overlooking 150 years of American practice, which had usually allowed local jurisdictions to control the local exercise of religion, the Court resurrected a phrase from a private letter of Thomas Jefferson to affirm that the Constitution erected "a wall of separation between church and state." Using this Jeffersonian guideline, the Court created standards aimed at preventing anything that could be considered the establishment of religion anywhere in the country.[30]

This one area of adjudication spoke for a general trend. Without a federal judiciary that was increasingly willing to act against local and regional instances of civil rights abuse—as well as on much else—the sustained progress of the movement was unthinkable.

A broad social development very much related to the expansion of central government activity was the transformation of popular communications by the electronic mass media. From 1926 to 1946, the number of American households with radio sets leapt from 4.5 million to 34 million; from 1946 to 1956, the number of families with televisions jumped from 8,000 to almost 35 million, and these numbers have continued to skyrocket.[31] For politics, the effects of television have been frequently chronicled—campaigns that rely on television require vast sums of money and demand shorter, more emotive messages; electability increasingly depends less on party attachments than on photogenic presence; media feeding frenzies easily derail candidates—like Governor George Romney in 1967, Senator Ed Muskie in 1972, or Senator Howard Dean in 2004—who make embarrassing public gaffes on camera; special interests with money grow disproportionately important. The key point is not just that television has fundamentally altered American politics. Rather, communications provides another instance where national perceptions, featuring highly charged electronic images, have replaced local loyalties featuring face-to-face political organization as the key to national electoral success. In the president election of 1960 it was widely held that John F. Kennedy's narrow margin of victory over Richard M. Nixon was supplied by the fresher appearance he projected during national television debates. That judgment has been disputed, but no one disputes that television has made a dramatic difference in the outworking of American electoral politics. Nor does anyone seriously doubt that, in the religious sphere, mastery of the airwaves has provided some leaders—like Oral Roberts, Billy Graham, Pat Robertson, or Dr. James Dobson—with unusual national visibility and, in some cases, substantial political clout.

Fully functioning national media, with the ability to transmit images in real time from anywhere to anywhere, were prerequisites for impressing the nation with the extent of civil rights abuses. Equally important was national coverage of the responses that civil rights leaders and followers made to those abuses.

Also of immense importance was the unprecedented economic boom that followed World War II. This boom accelerated a long-standing migration from farms to cities, even as it opened increased economic opportunity for a wide swath of Americans in a wide range of places.[32] The spread of mechanized agriculture throughout the South was one of the deep background changes that bore most directly on the civil rights movement. Reduced need for sharecroppers meant that redundant black laborers moved to the cities of the South, where some contributed to the man- and woman-power responsible for initiatives like the Montgomery Bus Boycott. Rural economic redundancy also increased black migration to northern cities, where more subtle patterns of race discrimination, as well as more space for black church growth, both resulted.[33] For portions of the South's governing and business elites, the rise of mechanization also made it possible to imagine a less restrictive social structure, since the economic system that seemed to require a large and subservient black peonage was passing away.

The great expansion of the suburbs was another result of postwar economic growth. It was fueled, literally, by a burgeoning industry of automobile production and massive federal subsidies for roads, highways, and suburb-to-city mass transit. The effects of suburbanization bore less directly, but no less powerfully, on the civil rights movement. The new suburbs were mostly free of the legal forms of discrimination that had existed in cities and the rural South; they were home to several generations of idealistic youth and conscientious elders who provided recruits and some financial support for civil rights activities. But they also could easily become de facto white enclaves that stymied the expansion of civil rights reforms by economic and social segmentation instead of judicial and legislative fiat.[34] Economic realities are harder to coordinate with ideological, religious, and social realities than with political realities, but only gnostics would deny the strong links between civil rights reform and the United States' powerful, but also multivalent, economic history.

A different sort of background for the civil rights movement was provided by the noncontroversial acceptance in the 1950s of salient religious language to define the American national purpose.[35] This willingness came from a broadly shared consensus that the worldwide struggle against "godless communism" demanded a countervailing assertion of America's religious character. Thus, in rapid order Congress in 1954 added the phrase "under God" to the national pledge of allegiance; it passed legislation in 1955 to put the phrase "In God We Trust" on the nation's currency (and issued an eight-cent stamp with that motto to mark this legislation); in that same year a new musical rendition of the pledge, including the phrase "under God," was performed by the Singing Sergeants of the United States Air Force before the House of Representatives (almost the last time it was sung in public); and in 1956 President Eisenhower affixed his signature to Public Law 84-851, which made "In God We Trust" the official motto of the United States.[36]

These initiatives were not meant to define the nation's religion precisely but were instead intended to enlist as many citizens as possible for a broad set of generically American values. They were opposed at the time only by fringe groups like the Unitarian Ministers Association and the Freethinkers of America. Soon, however, they became objects of contention when more and more people took offense at what they considered intrusive governmental meddling in private religious affairs, even as more and more people took offense at the manifest failure of American society to live up to the high ideals proclaimed in the newly ratified national religious slogans.

For the civil rights movement, this deployment of theistic language had mixed implications. On the one side, it eased the way for the movement's own direct use of explicitly Christian language for its own public purposes. On the other side, it allowed opponents of the movement to label any expansion of government authority, including expansion to secure civil rights, as a communist assault on both God and country. Quite apart from problems caused by blurring the line between religion and civil religion, the heightened use of religious language for purposes of national self-definition all but assured a more volatile, more passionate, and more broadly influential debate over the civil rights movement itself.

Other important changes in American society doubtless also provided significant context for civil rights reforms. For example, the great postwar expansion of higher education supported the movement in several ways: as a source of expanded opportunity for some blacks, as a site for conflict over desegregation, and as a broad force for national intellectual secularization. Other social developments that should be considered in order to explain modern civil rights history do not, however, have the general significance of the changed scope of federal authority, changes in the media, changes in the economy, and changes in the ritualized language of national self-identification.

The Centrality of Religion

Yet among other causes and effects, religious causes and effects were arguably most important. At this point I am seconding the general interpretation provided by David Chappell in his landmark study, *A Stone of Hope: Prophetic*

Religion and the Death of Jim Crow.[37] Its conclusion about
the centrality of religious factors in the success of the civil
rights movement of the 1950s and 1960s rests on four persuasively documented subarguments.

First, black prophetic religion in the powerful combination of elite and populist forms was singularly influential.
One of the strongest points in Chappell's general portrait is
his contention that the political and theological liberalism
undergirding northern mainline Protestants and secular political leaders did not have the capacity to jolt the nation into
acting aggressively on civil rights. Political and theological
liberals did consistently express their opposition to racial
injustice and did express their hopes for full civil rights.
But in judgments that are mine as much as Chappell's, the
opposition and the hope were politically weak because they
were normatively askew. The liberal view of evil was too
shallow to take the measure of racist sins; liberal expectations for human progress based on education and good will
were too feeble to overcome the entrenched antipathies of
a racially riven society; and liberal confidence in the ability
of enlightened social managers to remodel American mores
suffered from a blithe underestimation of the problem.

Besides African-American religion and liberal political
faith, the only other candidates that might have mobilized
sufficient zeal to stimulate broad-based social change were
the Catholic Church and the diverse congeries of white
evangelical and fundamentalist Protestants. While the
Catholic Church did enjoy notable advocates of civil rights
reform, centers of Catholic culture in the United States at
least into the 1960s remained the urban parishes where advocacy for civil rights met stiff resistance from the strongly
communal life that several generations of white Catholics
had painstakingly constructed for their churches, schools,

and community organizations.[38] For their part, white evangelicals and fundamentalists began to experience some intellectual, spiritual, and even social renewal during and after World War II. But they were still mostly inert with respect to almost all social and political issues, except their support for the West's battle against world communism.[39] Chappell, in other words, is correct: to blast loose the log-jam of restricted rights for black Americans, the only charge that could, and did, prevail was the detonation provided by African-American prophetic religion.

Second, Chappell is also convincing when he argues that white Christian elites—mainline Protestants, evangelical Protestants, and Roman Catholics—for the most part either accepted or actively promoted civil rights. It is, for example, a startling fact that the South's two most powerful regional denominations went on record as early as the *mid-1950s* to support national moves toward desegregation and urge peaceful compliance with them.[40] The Presbyterian Church in the United States, which had been formed in the early years of the Civil War by uniting different Presbyterian subgroups in the Confederacy, took this step even before the Supreme Court issued *Brown v. Board of Education* in 1954. The Southern Baptist Convention, which arose even earlier in 1844 when churches south of the Mason-Dixon Line insisted that missionaries could own slaves, made its statement shortly after *Brown*. Northern Protestant denominations and leading voices in the Catholic Church were even more consistently forthright than these strongly evangelical southern denominations.

For their part, the loosely organized networks of evangelical organizations were somewhat slower to promote civil rights. A very few evangelicals, like Frank Gaebelein, longtime rector of a New York private school and associate editor of *Christianity Today* magazine, personally took part in at least some aspects of the movement.[41] Some stood on the other side, like L. Nelson Bell, a founding editor of *Christianity Today* who in the mid-1950s held that "to force social contacts, in the name of Christianity, where such contacts are not desired, can compound our problems; not solve them."[42] But for nondenominational evangelicals, the quiet work of Bell's son-in-law, Billy Graham, who desegregated his evangelistic crusades in the 1950s, eventually won wide support for at least aspects of civil rights reform.[43] In a relatively short period, most of the major evangelical spokespersons moved to the moderate center on most racial issues.[44] Throughout the whole religious world, in sum, leading denominations and significant leaders of parachurch organizations did not impede the civil rights movement, and sometimes they actively promoted it.

Third, a most controversial contention in Chappell's *Stone of Hope* is the assertion that, while significant religious resistance did arise to oppose civil rights, the religion of this resistance was populist, unsupported by elite authority, and therefore limited in its effect.[45] This claim, though involving a number of complicated judgments, is still persuasive, even if the impact of populist, religiously driven prejudice was strong and often untroubled by guidance from elites.

Comparisons with the religious situation during the Civil War and the subsequent white supremacist "redemption" of the South help focus the issue. Whatever the religious support arrayed against the modern civil rights movement, such support was demonstrably weaker than the religious convictions that had defended the legitimacy of slavery and backed the reimposition of white rule. On the question of the Bible, for instance, arguments in the antebellum period were evenly matched, or even tilted toward those who defended slavery on the basis of Scripture.[46] During the civil rights era, by contrast, the contest was definitely one-sided. Popular belief in the Curse of Ham from Genesis, chapter 9, did enjoy considerable currency among those who held out for segregation.[47] But there was no recognized public spokesperson who gained any traction from that ancient text, in large part because all recognized Bible scholars, including defenders of segregation, acknowledged that the Genesis passage had nothing to do with modern racial groups. A few segregationists did make use of a phrase from Acts 17:26 (God "determined . . . the bounds of their habitation"), but they were easily trumped, as we saw earlier with Fannie Lou Hamer, by quoting the first part of that verse (God "hath made of one blood all nations of men for to dwell on all the face of the earth").

In some measure, popular religion no doubt fueled the violence that accompanied resistance to civil rights.[48] But Chappell makes a telling observation that, as terrible as the era's many murders, beatings, and other acts of physical intimidation were, they did not escalate into religion-sanctioned carnage on the scale of the Civil War. Violence against civil rights workers, and, even more pervasively, against African Americans who suffered serious economic and physical reprisals for joining the struggle, remains the great twentieth-century contradiction to the United States' self-proclaimed standard of "liberty and justice for all." But this violence was usually held in check, often by the same elite elements in southern white communities that had justified the Civil War with religious warrants. Some segregationists chose not to resist civil rights legislation and court orders; other southern whites spoke and acted for the new order. In a word, division within white ranks on race was much more pronounced than it had been before the Civil

War or during and after Reconstruction. Such division, which, among other things, reflected an altered religious landscape, made the warfare of the mid-nineteenth century impossible in the mid-twentieth.

Again, while resistance to civil rights was propelled by deep religious beliefs, this religion was not what the major churches defined as their faith. As fine studies of the Southern Baptists by Wayne Flynt and Mark Newman have shown, the influential Southern Baptist Convention included many members who were reluctant to support civil rights, but the denomination never produced articulate, theological, or principled leadership against racial equality.[49] It did number quite a few significant leaders who accepted or even advocated the new order.

If there were a few spokespeople for religious resistance to civil rights, none of them had the cultural authority that proslavery figures like James Henley Thornwell and Robert Louis Dabney had exercised before the Civil War. The influential Southern Baptist pastor W. A. Criswell of Dallas was representative of quite a few others. In 1956 he defended segregation in a speech before the South Carolina legislature, even though the speech contained no references to the Bible. Twelve years later, however, Criswell endorsed a statement by the annual meeting of the Southern Baptist Convention that, in the wake of the assassination of Martin Luther King, Jr., committed the denomination to end segregation in churches and housing and to support full civil rights for all American citizens. At the same time Criswell went on record to repudiate the use of the Bible to defend segregation.[50] In sum, from a historical perspective that takes account of American racism from the beginnings, the comparative focus of David Chappell's rendering of the modern civil rights movement is especially impressive.

The aspect of Chappell's argument that is open to the most serious challenge is a fourth contention that religiously driven, anti–civil rights sentiment was a force that did not long survive and has not exerted substantial continuing influence. Here careful research in broader connections among race, religion, and politics by several scholars has revealed a picture of great complexity. A whole range of forceful studies has shown both that overt, religiously derived resistance to civil rights did in fact fade rapidly in the 1970s, but also that the political resurgence of conservative Republicanism, with signal surges under Richard Nixon, Ronald Reagan, and George W. Bush, was in some measure a response to the advance of civil rights. The nature of that tangled relationship is the subject of the next chapter.

On the civil rights movement itself, it is appropriate to conclude that, while religion was not the only factor explaining its development and partial success, it was nonetheless a crucial factor throughout. The easiest thing to document is the strength of the African-American religion that drove the movement. The hardest thing to gauge is the relative strength or weakness of religious factors in the white population that accepted or impeded civil rights. No responsible political history can afford to neglect nonreligious factors. Equally, no political account of the era that does not foreground black religion and ponder carefully the place of religion in the wider society can be considered historically responsible.

CHAPTER V

The Civil Rights Movement as the Fulcrum of Recent Political History

The quarter century from 1955 to 1980 witnessed unusually complex connections for the nexus of race, religion, and politics. If it is reasonably clear how the politics of the civil rights era grew out of the unfinished business of the Civil War and Reconstruction (1865–1955), and also reasonably clear how the politics of the recent past emerged out of the civil rights era (1980–2004), the major puzzles for historical analysis lie in between. Oceans of verbiage, along with substantial islands of firm scholarship, define the landscape of interpretation for the United States' recent political history. The narrative that follows draws on some of that scholarship but has probably been too much influenced by the not always responsible floods of journalistic punditry on religion in contemporary American society.

The "values voting" in 2004, which was widely held to have produced the reelection of Republican George W. Bush over his Democratic opponent, Senator John Kerry from Massachusetts, by itself sparked a literary explosion.[1] So impressed—or disconcerted, or amazed, or panicked—was the nation's intellectual sector with the results of this election and the deepening religious influences it was thought to reflect that publishers rushed entire subgenres of books into print—one set to explain (and often to combat) the political consequences of the Bush campaign's successful appeal to white evangelical Protestants,[2] another to probe the character of these same evangelical Protestants,[3] and a third to revisit questions about the role of religion in the nation's past that in this climate had again become controversial.[4]

Behind this recent flurry of near-instant commentary lies a weightier set of deeply researched academic studies on connections among race, religion, and politics.[5] These sober studies are backed by an even broader array of other serious works that, if some may stint on religion, nonetheless offer a great deal of carefully distilled wisdom on recent U.S. political history.[6] My effort here takes advantage of this scholarship as it traces the themes of this book over the last half century—race in connection with religion, race in connection with the exercise of government power, and religion in connection with politics. It is not an iron-clad demonstration of historical certainty. It is a plausible final chapter to a story that stretches back from the twenty-first century to the decades before the Civil War.

The Civil Rights Movement as a Spark

This final chapter begins in 1954 with the Supreme Court's decision in *Brown v. Board of Education* that overturned the "separate but equal" provisions of *Plessy v. Ferguson* and mandated the integration of public schools "with all deliberate speed." White religious reaction to this decision was mixed. Some applauded, some resisted, more found themselves nervous about the speed, means, and agents of judicially mandated integration. As a goad for, and reflection of, contemporary sentiment, *Brown* showed that an increased number of Americans seemed willing to question whether morality or religion really did support the persistent racist division of American society. But change in response to the Supreme Court's decision moved slowly, with flashes of violence in the South (as at Little Rock in 1957) and almost no attention to the de facto segregation of public education in many northern cities.[7]

Into the fractured force field created by *Brown* and reactions to it—and alongside the general increase of federal mandates for civil rights—came the well-publicized events of late 1955 that transformed cautious judicial evolution into political revolution. It is, by now, a story often told. On December 1, 1955, in Montgomery, Alabama, Rosa Parks, a black forty-two-year-old seamstress, refused to give up her seat on a public bus when asked to do so by a white man. When she was arrested and then found guilty of violating Alabama's law that prohibited racially integrated seating in public transportation, Montgomery's black community mounted a boycott of the local bus system. A leader of the boycott was the young Baptist minister, Martin Luther King, Jr. What followed, through a complicated and often ironic series of events, was not only the achievement of civil rights reform, but also the political mobilization of white evangelical America, the expansion of a much more aggressively secular nation, the reshaping of political and religious demography, the intensification of religious rhetoric in presidential orations, and a whole lot more.

The case involving Rosa Parks eventually reached the Supreme Court, which in November 1956 followed its earlier judgment on public schooling by ruling that racial segregation on public transportation was illegal. By that time the public phase of the civil rights movement—which drew so powerfully on black religious traditions—was well and truly launched. In responding to the initiatives of the movement, the power of central government eventually expanded considerably beyond the limits reached during the New Deal. It soon was touching directly an increasing number of institutions and practices that had structured the daily lives of American citizens for more than a century.

It is important to remember the sequence of events that led to this result. Despite indications in the 1960 presidential campaign that he was prepared to act on civil rights, President Kennedy did virtually nothing until he delivered a hastily thrown together television address on June 11, 1963, in which he defined the need for comprehensive civil rights legislation as "a moral issue . . . as old as the Scriptures and . . . as clear as the American Constitution." Kennedy moved when he did, however, because of intense pressures brought on by graphic media coverage of a host of dramatic events precipitated by civil rights activism. His speech made the connections plan: "The events in Birmingham and elsewhere have so increased the cries for equality that no city or state or legislative body can prudently choose to ignore them."[8] Even a partial record of those events is stunning:[9]

- Rioting in October 1962 at the University of Mississippi in reaction to efforts at enrolling James Meredith as the first black student at that school.

- Imprisonment in April 1963 of Martin Luther King, Jr., and several associates in Birmingham for their peaceful efforts to register black voters.

- Violent attacks by police dogs and fire hoses in May 1963 against demonstrators in Birmingham.

- And on the day of Kennedy's speech, a tense stand-off at the University of Alabama when federal marshals forced Governor George Wallace to admit the first two black students at that institution.

But even with Kennedy's initiative in June 1963, it is almost inconceivable that the segregationist and small-government lock on the United States Congress could have been broken without another full year of dramatic events precipitated by aggressive civil rights reformers and violent reactions to some of them:

- The assassination, on the night of Kennedy's June speech, of Medgar Evers, field secretary of the NAACP in Mississippi, who was gunned down in front of his own Jackson home.

- The massive March on Washington for Jobs and Freedom on August 28, 1963, during which Martin Luther King, Jr., delivered his famous speech, "I have a dream."

- The bombing of the Sixteenth Street Baptist Church in Birmingham on September 15, 1963, in which three young black girls were killed just as they arrived for Sunday School.

- The assassination of President Kennedy on November 22, 1963, and the immediate decision by his successor, Lyndon Johnson, to make passage of a civil rights bill his central homage to the slain president.

- Aggressive public speech-making and even more aggressive private arm-twisting by President Johnson over more than half a year to secure passage of the civil rights bill despite the determined opposition of southern senators and representatives.

- The announcement in June 1964 that three civil rights volunteers in Mississippi were missing and feared murdered by white terrorists.

Then, and only then, did Congress pass the landmark Civil Rights Act of 1964, which President Johnson signed into law on July 2, 1964.

The well-publicized chain of events making possible the passage of the Voting Rights Act of 1965 (signed August 6) was just as dramatic: anguished wrangling at the Democratic National Convention over whether to seat the Mississippi Freedom Democratic Party or the whites-only delegation of the regular Democrats, a landslide victory by Lyndon Johnson over Barry Goldwater in the presidential election of 1964 and an accompanying huge Democratic majority in Congress, the five-day Selma-to-Montgomery march for voting rights that was delayed by a brutal attack from Alabama State Police on marchers in Selma, and further intensive lobbying by President Johnson.

Civil rights legislation became the law of the land when well-publicized violence against self-sacrificing civil rights proponents compelled the federal government to act. What Kevin Kruse has written about the racial situation in Atlanta was true for the nation as a whole: "The civil rights bill of 1964 proved, without question, that active intervention by the federal government was essential for the success of the civil rights movement. . . . Without its involvement, the racial impasse in Atlanta and countless other communities might never have been solved."[10]

This expansion of federal power, it is important to underscore, came in response to African-American reformers who did not hide their religion: they believed in the intractability of evil, they defined the struggle for justice as a religious imperative, and they looked for "prophetic Christianity" to break through the toils of dehumanizing segregation. The contrast with the American Civil War came fully into play at this point. In the 1850s a full range of southern theologians boldly defended slavery as sanctioned by Christian theology and justified by specific texts of Scripture. Their religious arguments nerved a whole section of the country to secede, to fight, and to die for the cause. In the 1950s southern segregationists clung to legal precedence but could not—or would not—make a convincing appeal to religion in defense of their position. They were led, not by learned and respected clergy, but by populist pols.

Another major difference was the instantaneous media coverage. Images of demonstrators kneeling to pray in the streets or being inspired by scriptural phrases offered a powerful contrast to images of snarling guard dogs and obese policemen directing fire hoses onto peaceful demonstrators. Whatever the legal complexities, television in the years 1955 to 1964 made the civil rights advocates look good and the defenders of segregation look very, very bad.

In contrast to the general theism of anticommunism, the civil rights movement brought particularistic Christianity back into the center of American politics. It reinvigorated the possibility that some moral principles deserved higher loyalty than the established law of the land. It linked a traditional Christian vocabulary of moral righteousness with

the shift in religion

a liberal political vocabulary of individual right. It showed how well-organized movements could carry their message to a vast audience through the modern mass media. It forsook the pursuit of consensus for the practice of confrontation. And it was successful in pressing the government to pass new legislation and reverse judicial traditions. Because of what the advocates of civil rights did, the expansion of judicial and legislative power to end segregation eventually came to seem instinctively right to most Americans for many reasons, religious as well as political. Comparatively considered, government action on civil rights was accepted more readily than would have been possible for any other problem not connected with the nation's troubled racial history.

The nascent civil rights movement was thus an opening wedge in the transformation of American religion and politics.[11] The deluge of the 1960s soon followed.

Things Up for Grabs

A serious literature now exists to show that the welter of upsetting social developments lumped together as "the '60s" involved complex currents whose full effects may not have been felt until well into the next decade.[12] Yet the stereotype is still useful. If one thinks of "the '60s" as lasting from the Bay of Pigs invasion in 1961 to the resignation of President Richard Nixon in 1974 or the withdrawal of American troops from Vietnam in 1975, we still have a great concentration of traumatic events in a relatively short period: assassination of three national leaders; nuclear face-down over Cuba; increasingly controversial military involvement in Vietnam; construction of the Berlin Wall; lingering violence directed at civil rights workers; race riots in Los Angeles, Detroit, Newark, and other urban centers; student riots in protest of the Vietnam War; economic uncertainty and the worst recession since the Great Depression; a sudden relaxation of censorship for books, plays, and movies; and the resignation under fire of a president—and all piped into the nation's living rooms in living color.

In overly simple terms, "the '60s" strained conventional standards—for public propriety, the family, and much more. It was a time of violent public confrontations over foreign policy, social policy, and political decisions. These years witnessed an ever-expanding series of well-publicized challenges to what once had seemed fixed American certainties. For some citizens it was an exhilarating period of liberation, for others a terrifying period of impending doom, and for still more simply a vast confusion. For those who felt particularly aggrieved, inspired, threatened, or empowered, it was a time of political quickening. Particularly for large numbers of white evangelicals, located especially in the South, Midwest, and Southwest, it was also a period of unusual distress. To them it seemed that this "one nation under God" was being stolen away right in front of their eyes. Soon many white evangelicals, along with increasing numbers of Roman Catholics, thought they had figured out who was responsible for stealing their nation away.

The growing reality of actual violence, actual crime, and actual sexual "liberation"—combined with media hype over violence, crime, and sexual "liberation"—created a psychological climate that, for many Americans, transformed the prospect of political change into a direct personal threat. Midst a welter of political change, the most far-reaching was federally mandated civil rights reform.

An Expanded Federal Presence

In 1964 the Civil Rights Act went far beyond the tentative provisions of a similarly named bill from 1957, though the earlier measure had been important for breaking the logjam preventing any federal action on civil rights since Reconstruction. The 1964 legislation banned all discrimination in public accommodations and in hiring, created the Equal Employment Opportunity Commission to enforce the act, and authorized the withholding of federal funds from public programs that discriminated. That same year witnessed final passage of the Twenty-fourth Amendment, which banned poll taxes, one of the chief devices keeping black people unregistered. In 1965 followed the Voting Rights Act, which stipulated federal monitors and, if necessary, direct federal intervention to ensure the right to vote for all American citizens. Ninety-five years after the passage of the Fifteenth Amendment, its promise of an open franchise for all would at last be fulfilled. (The impact was felt almost immediately: in the presidential election of 1968 there were 3.6% more popular votes cast than in 1964, although in nineteen northern and western states the totals were actually lower in 1968 than in 1964. By contrast, voting participation increased 10% in Georgia, 17% in Texas, 18% in Florida, 22% in Louisiana, 27% in South Carolina, 31% in Virginia, 52% in Alabama, and 60% in Mississippi.[13]) In 1968 Congress passed legislation forbidding discrimination in selling or renting homes, which resulted in easier minority access to previously all-white neighborhoods as well as considerable white apprehension about rapid changes in the character of local neighborhoods. Never in the nation's history did government act so fast to remedy so many wrongs.

This unprecedented burst of civil rights legislation and the serious efforts to enforce it with federal agencies was greeted by a barrage of outrage. Leaders of the chorus were diehard segregationists. Yet they expressed their outrage not so much in racial terms, as with a republican rhetoric emphasizing traditional American fears of centralized power and traditional solicitude for local control of local affairs. Their aim was defense of "states' rights" and the "restoration of local government." The fear was of "federal dictatorship," "despotic . . . arbitrary . . . dictatorial" government, "omnivorous federal government," "oppressive liberal government," "federal occupation," "federal intervention," "the trend of socialism," "a totalitarian blueprint designed by socialists in Washington," " big government," and, endlessly, "communism."[14] Such responses to civil rights legislation were extreme when they were uttered; today they seem simply absurd.

The rhetoric at the time, however, was not so absurd, and for an obvious reason: the federal government that was expanding its reach into the daily life of citizens on civil rights was at the same time expanding its reach on a host of other matters as well. The precipitating force of the civil rights movement on American politics in general was never just a question of civil rights. It was always also a question of context, of events taking place alongside civil rights reforms. For the attention of the federal government to civil rights, the primary political context was sharply increased attention to everything else.

Most intrusive was the draft for military service that was affecting more and more young men even as public sentiment turned decisively against the war in Vietnam that draftees were being asked to fight. Significantly, through all of the growing federal attention to civil rights, from the mid-1950s to the mid-1970s, the pull of responsibility (or damage control) in Vietnam was an ever-present counter-point to domestic controversies.

More obviously well-meaning in intent were greatly ex-panded federal aid to education (the National Defense Ed-ucation Act of 1964, and from 1965 the Elementary and Secondary Education Act and the Higher Education Act), greatly expanded federal health assistance (and manage-ment) through Medicare, greatly expanded numbers of new arrivals because of the Immigration Reform Bill of 1965, greatly expanded attention to the environment, and greatly expanded efforts to help the poor (the War on Poverty). Lyndon Johnson is often given credit (or blame) for the great expansion of federal scope entailed by his Great So-ciety programs. But John F. Kennedy's adventures in Cuba and Vietnam, as also Richard Nixon's willingness to use federal power in new ways (like price controls to combat inflation), illustrated the same pattern.

Quite apart from the history of civil rights, in other words, the Kennedy-Johnson-Nixon years witnessed an ex-traordinary increase in the range of federal activities, and all predicated on the belief in the effectiveness of federal power. Charges of rampant Big Government, which from segregationists were a smokescreen for white supremacy, became more honestly debatable for a much larger popula-tion when they came in response to other federal reforms.

Spin-offs

Another major difficulty associated with civil rights reforms compounded concern over the general growth of govern-ment. This second arena of controversy took shape in the wake of those reforms, but with atmospheric rather than direct connections. The difficulty came from the growing suspicion among many citizens that agitation for civil rights was organically related to other agitations for a whole catalogue of new rights. The rationale for civil rights reform grew out of the long, long history of American racist discrimination. By contrast, the rationale for most of the other reforms grew out of very modern circumstances. But if logical connections were weak between civil rights reform and aggressive claims for other rights, both proponents and opponents often took a close link for granted.[15]

From the mid-1960s, for example, the civil rights movement as a whole was undercut when observers perceived the actions and words of black nationalists, black separatists, black criminals, and black looters as somehow of a piece with the Montgomery Bus Boycott, the Freedom Riders, the Mississippi Freedom Summer, and the Selma-to-Montgomery march for voting rights in Alabama. These and other demonstrations sponsored by the Southern Christian Leadership Conference (SCLC) and like-minded local groups were guided by nonviolent principles that their promoters articulated in explicitly Christian, Gandhian, and American democratic terms. On the very few occasions when nonviolent protests led to violence from the demonstrators—as in the Memphis sanitation workers strike immediately before the assassination of Martin Luther King, Jr.,—leaders of the SCLC labored with all their energy to repudiate the use of violence. If the white opponents of integration were, in fact, the ones who set the precedent for interracial violence, it was the civil rights movement that suffered from the stigma of violent rhetoric and the damaging riots in central cities of the mid-1960s.

When King, James Bevel, Julian Bond, and other civil rights leaders came out against the Vietnam War, it was again a case where civil rights goals were in many minds elided with a particular stance on U.S. foreign policy. To

King and his associates, the nonviolent principles of civil rights reform mandated a position against this war. But not to Lyndon Johnson who, even as he escalated American investment in the war, remained staunchly committed to racial equality. Nor to many moderate and conservative Americans who retained doubts about the civil rights movement even as they supported the war as necessary for the battle against world communism. Strongly felt religion crept back into the equation on these issues since patriotic sentiments, whether for or against the war, were often closely tied to foundational religious values. Support for civil rights did not necessarily entail opposition to the Vietnam War, but in the minds of many the righteousness, or stigma, of the one stuck to the other.

The free speech movement that blossomed in the 1960s at Berkeley, California, was similarly associated with civil rights reform. The key Berkeley agitator, Mario Savio, like a few other early leaders of the movement, began his efforts on behalf of free speech at Berkeley in the fall of 1964 just after he returned from a summer as a voting rights volunteer in Mississippi.[16] The free speech protests against the Vietnam War and against restrictions on public utterance were, therefore, tied closely enough to campaigns for racial equality that protesters against the protesters almost naturally condemned anti-Vietnam, pro–free speech, and pro–civil rights agitations as parts of one whole. Ronald Reagan, then in the process of shifting his career from acting to politics, became the most notable spokesperson for that antiprotester protest. With masterful speech making, Reagan disavowed racism while he attacked a bundle of reforms, including civil rights reforms. Many Americans found even more convincing his identification of an expanding federal government as the culprit behind the reforms-gone-wrong.

Women's rights were inserted into the Civil Rights Act of 1964 as a segregationist ploy. Southern senators felt that they would have a stronger chance of filibustering the bill to death if it contained prohibitions against discrimination for reasons of gender as well as of race. The ploy did not work. In fact, it boomeranged when alert advocates of the nascent feminist movement parlayed moral revulsion against racial discrimination into a broadly effective promotion of equal rights for women. It is striking that all of the civil rights leaders used highly gendered language (as did virtually everyone else in that period). The fact that today it has become conventional to write and speak with gender-neutral terms testifies to the spin-off force from the civil rights movement. Feminists recognized the movement as opening a door for women, which they walked through successfully, despite the fact that this development was virtually unanticipated even by the few female participants in civil rights leadership.

Not the least of the unintended consequences of effective mobilization of Christian language for civil rights was the use of very similar language by those who mobilized to form the New Christian Right.[17] The latter mobilization trailed the anti-Vietnam, free speech, and feminist movements, but when it appeared, its vocabulary was strongly reminiscent of the vocabulary that drove the civil rights movement. Biblical phrases, traditional Christian verities reworked for contemporary problems, energetic organization on the model of religious voluntary associations, and, not least, selective use of religious imperatives—all were Christian conservative tactics that followed the path of civil rights reform.

Even later, leaders of gay rights movements would make explicit use of the methods, principles, and vocabulary of the civil rights movement as they made their own claim on the American public. As Taylor Branch has put this connection, "within decades, human energies founded on the civil rights movement would obliterate much of this lethal stigma [of homosexuality] and lift nearly all the closeted silence."[18]

In a word, the civil rights movement was transformative *as a movement* perhaps almost as much as it was in its campaign for civil rights. Some Americans have seen the circles expanding from the civil rights center as a natural consequence, others as a perversion. In the perspective of recent history, it is indisputable that civil rights reform, though rooted securely in opposition to racial discrimination, became in the tumult of the times much, much more than just an appeal for racial justice. In the longer historical view, it is just as indisputable that ingredients contributing to the many political explosions that began in the 1960s had been stored up over a very long period of national failure to deal with racial inequality.

The larger historical point is the realization of how much came to be packed into the charged category of "civil rights." When reaction came, therefore, it came in response not just to reform on racial issues, but also to the general expansion of federal authority and to the "rights revolutions" spreading out in the wake of civil rights reforms. In addition, when reaction to these larger developments took place, much of that reaction was phrased in fervent religious terms almost as strong as the fervent religion of the civil rights movement.

The movement and all that was connected to it by way of expansion, or by way of opposition, precipitated epochal political change. For his own study of race and suburbanization, Kevin Kruse catalogued the momentous implications:

> the demise of white supremacy and the rise of white suburbia; the fragmentation of old liberal coalitions and the construction of new conservative ones; the contested relationship between the federal government and state and local entities; the debates over the public realm and the private; the struggle over the distribution of money and the sharing of power; the competing claims to basic rights and responsibilities of citizenship; and, of course, conflicts rooted in divisions of generation, class, and, above all, race.[19]

The depth and extent of the change that Kruse and many others have identified can be seen in how they were reflected in unprecedented shifts of geographical and religious political allegiance.

The New Deal had earlier brought a great political alteration, but one that affected the whole nation with relative uniformity. The implementation of social security, government regulation of financial markets and energy, provision for union organizing, and other products of the New Deal were important because, with modest variation, they affected the nation as a whole. Yet before and after the New Deal, the relative political allegiance of the country's regions remained mostly what it had been before. With the exception of a move by African Americans (mostly Protestants) to the Democratic Party, the basic adherence of religious groups remained the same.

By contrast, the political realignment brought about by the civil rights movement and the various reactions to it worked at a different level. They affected regions of the country differently; they involved the enfranchisement of a whole new class of citizens; they inverted party identifications that had been stable for most of a century; they have featured extreme, Manichaean political controversy; and because religion has been so intimately a part of this realignment, they have has also multiplied visceral emotions more widely than all other political realignments in American history except those occasioned by the Civil War and Reconstruction. Because, in other words, the realignment that has been under way since the 1950s involves the powerful combination of race and religion, it has penetrated deeply into the consciousness of the body politic.

The geographic realignment has been the most obvious result. In a much reported comment, President Lyndon Johnson told Bill Moyers immediately after signing the Civil Rights Act of 1964: "It is an important gain, but I think I just delivered the South to the Republican Party for a long time to come."[20] Johnson was thinking about what federal civil rights enforcement would do to the Democratic Party's racially based hegemony in the South, and he was dead on target. As figure 5.1 (p. 154) indicates, civil rights triggered the reversal of regional political loyalties that had remained in place since the 1850s.

Neither President Johnson nor other observers in the 1960s, however, could have foreseen how much the forces connected to civil rights reform would alter the nation's political demography of religion. As table 5.1 (p. 155) indicates, presidential voting by many significant religious groups has changed decisively in the last half century. White evangelicals have moved from being a swing group to become the backbone of Republican support. White Roman Catholics have moved from being strongly Democratic to

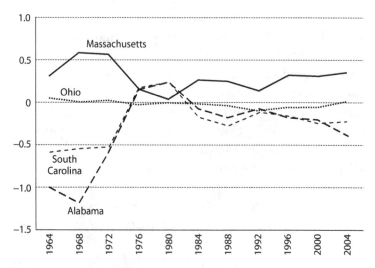

Figure 5.1. State Democratic Vote as Percentage of National Democratic Vote, 1964–2004

become a divided constituency. Black Protestants, strong for the Democrats since the middle of Franklin Roosevelt's tenure, have become decisively more Democratic. Mainline Protestant support for Republicans has remained firm, but with some decline in the twenty-first century. And the votes of those who do not practice any religion (seculars) have moved recently from marginally Democratic to strongly Democratic. For white evangelicals, white Catholics, and black Protestants, the pivot in presidential voting was the period 1960 to 1972, the same years in which regional voting allegiances were transformed. In both cases, civil rights—broadly construed—was the reason.

To account for white evangelical voting, including connections to the civil rights movement, requires an extended narrative. The Catholic picture is also complex, but for different reasons. Both cases, however, are of first importance

TABLE 5.1

Vote of Religious Segments of U.S. Population as a Percentage
Higher or Lower Than National Republican Vote

Year	White evangelical Protestants	White mainline Protestants	White Roman Catholics	Black Protestants	No religious affiliation (secular)
1936	0	33	−50	−3	−22
1940	2	29	−38	−16	−9
1944	0	25	−31	−33	−19
1948	−7	34	−39	n.a.	−10
1952	9	24	−16	−66	−3
1956	0	18	−8	−40	−12
1960	18	37	−67	−37	−12
1964	15	39	−33	−98	−3
1968	28	33	−26	−93	−15
1972	31	17	0	−75	−17
1976	4	31	−10	−85	−10
1980	16	25	4	−87	4
1984	28	24	−5	−81	−5
1988	30	21	−4	−85	−6
1992	47	21	−2	−79	−28
1996	43	17	−2	−77	−9
2000	48	20	0	−92	−28
2004	53	−2	4	−67	−45

Note: In 2004 the white evangelical vote polled 78% for George Bush vs. a national total of 51%; Bush's white evangelical vote was 153% of the national vote and so a score +53; in that same year the seculars voted 28% for Bush, or 55% of the national vote, so a score of −45.

Source: Adapted from information in Lyman Kellstedt et al., "Faith Transformed: Religion and American Politics from FDR to G. W. Bush," in *Religion and American Politics: From the Colonial Period to the Present*, 2nd ed., ed. Mark A. Noll and Luke Harlow (New York: Oxford University Press, 2007) , 269–95.

in charting the broader history of race, religion, and American politics.

Mobilization of White Evangelicals and the Rise of the Christian Right

For white evangelicals, the civil rights revolution was the key to changing attitudes about participating in politics as well as for the direction that this political action took. For the achievements of the movement—from *Brown v. Board of Education* and the first, hesitant federal civil rights bill in 1957, through the landmark legislation of the 1960s—there was at first little active white evangelical support. The early division of opinion among northern evangelicals is suggested by what was published in *Christianity Today*, the flagship evangelical journal founded by Billy Graham in 1956. Within a few weeks in early 1957, the magazine published material strongly supporting the Supreme Court in its push for integration, a detailed defense of some kinds of segregation as biblical, an editorial lamenting that it took the Supreme Court (instead of the churches) to highlight the evils of American racism, and many letters blasting the published defense of segregation.[21] But by the late 1960s and early 1970s, white evangelicals, even in the South, had mostly accepted the inevitability of civil rights for blacks, and some had even become active advocates of the new order.

Despite a lack of deep involvement in the civil rights movement, evangelicals were nevertheless affected in two significant ways. First, once legally enforced racism was gone, the great impediment that had restricted the influence of southern religion to only the South was also gone. Stripped of racist overtones, southern evangelical religion—the preaching, the piety, the sensibilities, and above all the music—became much easier to export throughout the country. Billy Graham had earlier shown how attractive a nonracist form of affective southern evangelicalism could be. As several historians, especially Darren Dochuk, have demonstrated, influential evangelicals from the South (Pat Robertson, D. James Kennedy, Bill Bright, Jerry Falwell, Anita Bryant, even Jimmy Carter and Bill Clinton) would find it much easier to export the gospel sensibilities of their region once that region was no longer stigmatized for its racism.[22]

The second effect of the civil rights movement for white evangelicals was political. With exceptions in some southern locales, the most important factor in realigning evangelical political allegiance throughout the nation was not race directly. It was rather the expansion of central governmental power that, to be sure, had been demonstrated forcibly in the enforcement of desegregation. As several sociologists, especially Robert Wuthnow, have shown, the great political complaint of modern evangelicals has been directed against what is perceived as a federally sponsored intrusion of alien moral norms into situations where local mores and local leaders had once dominated.[23] For some, this resentment began in the 1930s, with the New Deal. For more, it came to life in response to the expanded role of federal power on behalf of civil rights in the 1950s and 1960s. For even more, it arose in response to other federal initiatives undertaken in this same era. Especially critical was the fact that evangelicals perceived the national mandates imposed by the federal government in the wake of civil rights initiatives as offensive intrusions attacking the family, gender, and sex.

For the political history of evangelicals, it was telling that the first important civil rights initiatives of the 1950s took place at the same time that the federal government was sponsoring new science curricula as part of the effort to catch up with the Soviet Union after Sputnik. The unintended spin-off of these curricular intrusions was evangelical offense at the national promotion of evolution. Historians of science have shown that creation science was languishing in backwaters until the 1950s when federal promotion of the new curricula for elementary and secondary schools, which included presentation of evolutionary theories, brought creationism back to life.[24] The evangelical offense against evolution has never been precisely science; rather, it has always been more political resentment that tax dollars for public education were being used to inculcate teachings that seemed to overthrow what parents wanted their children to learn about God's presence in and behind the world.

Next, and following earlier court rulings that applied the Fourteenth Amendment to state laws and that discerned a constitutional wall of separation between church and state, the courts began vigorously to adjudicate many aspects of religion and public life that had hitherto been mostly left to the states. Some of the judgments expanded what it meant to practice religion freely, as in *Wisconsin v. Yoder* (1972), which exempted some Amish families from the public school laws of the state of Wisconsin. Other judgments expanded the new meaning of nonestablishment to exclude the recitation of prayers (1962) and scriptural devotional readings (1963) from the nation's public schools, regardless of local sentiments. At a stroke, conventions of Protestant practice, mostly in the Midwest and South, that had long been an accepted part of daily life were declared unconstitutional. The courts also plunged directly into cases concerning the public display of religious symbols, the activities of government-sponsored chaplains, the actions of voluntary religious groups in public schools, and the use of prayer at public gatherings. With rare exceptions, these decisions looked to white evangelicals like abuses of central government authority.

Then came *Roe v. Wade*. Ironically, major evangelical institutions like the Southern Baptist Convention and *Christianity Today* magazine were not particularly offended when the decision was announced in 1973. To them, abortion was still a mostly Catholic issue. As such, whatever nervousness evangelicals might have harbored about abortion-on-demand was for a brief period dampened by the instincts of historical Catholic-Protestant antagonism. But this situation did not last long. Rapidly improving relations between Catholic pro-life advocates and some evangelicals, as well as effective pro-life publicity from key evangelical leaders, especially the populist theologian, Francis Schaeffer, soon made anti-abortion into a foundation of evangelical political mobilization.[25] In the 1950s and 1960s, most evangelicals did not approve when a few states began to loosen abortion restrictions. But they were not galvanized into political action until the mid- to late 1970s when effective spokespersons defined the Supreme Court's mandate overturning the entire nation's legal restrictions on abortion as a moral disaster.

The Equal Rights Amendment, which was passed by Congress in 1972 (but not ratified by a sufficient number of states), became another occasion for worrying about centralized federal authority. It was again resisted by evangelicals as disruptive federal meddling with firmly settled gender traditions, and rejected even by evangelicals and Pentecostals whose denominations had pioneered in supporting the public ministry of women. In their thorough study of opposition to the amendment in North Carolina, Donald Mathews and

Jane De Hart found that opponents linked this federal proposal with other forces perceived as attacking the family:
"In a world where both the school and workplace had come
under federal scrutiny in unexpected ways, no one could
really guarantee that the institution in which gender roles
were defined and passed on—the family—would not come
under similar scrutiny." Especially when other agents also
seemed to be pushing in the same direction, "no one could
really guarantee that government would not intensify social
engineering under the Equal Rights Amendment." The key
matter at the base of opposition was clear: "Equality had
come to symbolize government manipulation of the weak, a
pretext for increasing the surveillance of an interventionist
state."[26]

Gay rights, which have been an object of intense publicity in recent years, posed further difficulty. Enough evangelicals have had personal experience with lesbians and
homosexuals in their own families, and enough evangelicals really do believe what they have said about separating
condemnation of behavior from acceptance of the person,
that gay issues may have remained only a midlevel concern,
were it not again for the perception that central authority
was imposing alien legal standards. The imposition of these
standards on matters concerning personal sexuality, marriage, and family formation has been particularly offensive
in light of the deeply engrained conviction, which is shared
by other Christian traditions, that issues of personal sexuality, marriage, and family formation are at the heart of faithful living before God.

Some commentators have suggested that concern over
the ruling of the Massachusetts Supreme Court that permit-
ted gay marriage was important in tilting the 2004 election
to George W. Bush.[27] If so, a clear link can be seen between

recent political divisions and early civil rights activities, but civil rights understood broadly as the groundwork for a "rights revolution" promoted by the nation's courts rather than narrowly as a struggle for racial justice.

If this reading of white evangelical mobilization on behalf of the Republican Party and right-wing causes is correct, race has not been the all-encompassing factor. Yet national attention to race and civil rights was the doorway through which evangelicals marched in their determination to rescue the nation.

The broader political significance of evangelical mobilization hangs also on the fact that, within the American religious world, evangelicals were becoming a much larger component at the very time they were mobilizing politically. In a broad development that has not been studied as thoroughly as it deserves, the numbers in Southern Baptist churches, independent congregations, churches associated with the Assemblies of God, the Seventh-Day Adventists, and conservative branches of the Presbyterians, Methodists, and Anglicans have expanded substantially, while the national proportion of mainline Protestants has declined. The political impact of these changes has meant that as Republican support softened among mainline Protestants, that decline was more than offset by rapid expansion of the evangelical constituents that have turned strongly to the GOP. Table 5.2 sets out some of the figures for church adherence that outline the scale of these changes. For the wider conjunctions relevant to a study of race, religion, and politics, the historical observations of sociologist Stephen Warner are significant:

> The profile of American congregations has changed in ... remarkable ways since the watershed year of

TABLE 5.2
Changes in Denominational Inclusive Membership,
ca. 1960–ca. 2005

Mostly white mainline Protestant	
Evangelical Lutheran Church in America*	down 310,000
Presbyterian Church (USA)	down 970,000
United Church of Christ*	down 980,000
Disciples of Christ	down 1,060,000
Episcopal Church in the United States	down 1,160,000
United Methodist Church*	down 2,460,000
Mostly white evangelical Protestant	
Salvation Army	up 170,000
International Church of the Foursquare Gospel	up 240,000
Church of the Nazarene	up 320,000
Christian and Missionary Alliance	up 360,000
Seventh-day Adventist	up 620,000
Church of God (Cleveland, Tenn.)	up 820,000
Assemblies of God	up 2,270,000
Southern Baptist Convention	up 6,540,000
For comparison	
Church of Jesus Christ of Latter-day Saints	up 4,110,000
Church of God in Christ (black Pentecostal)	up 5,110,000
Roman Catholic Church	up 25,720,000

U.S. population: ca. 178,000,000 (1960) to ca. 295,000,000 (2005)

Note: These figures do not include new, largely evangelical groups like the Vineyard Fellowship, the network of Calvary Chapels, or mega-church organizations (e.g., The Willow Creek Association) that did not exist in 1960.

* For the Evangelical Lutheran Church in America, the United Methodist Church, and the United Church of Christ, figures for 1960 include constituent denominations that merged to make up these churches.

Sources: Benson Y. Landis, ed., *Yearbook of American Churches for 1962* (New York: National Council of Churches, 1961); and Eileen W. Lindner, ed., *Yearbook of American and Canadian Churches, 2006* (Nashville: Abingdon, 2006).

TABLE 5.3

Presidential Vote Coalitions by Party and Religious Traditions,
1960, 1992, 2004 (percent of total party vote)

	1960		1992		2004	
	Rep.	Dem.	Rep.	Dem.	Rep.	Dem.
Evangelical Protestant	24	17	37	15	40	12
Mainline Protestant	58	25	23	16	18	19
Black Protestant	3	6	2	14	3	13
White Catholic	7	36	23	24	20	19
All others	3	10	7	18	11	15
Secular	5	6	8	13	8	22
Nationwide	100	100	100	100	100	100

Note: Rep. = Republican; Dem. = Democrat.

Source: Lyman Kellstedt et al., "Faith Transformed: Religion and American Politics from FDR to G. W. Bush," in *Religion and American Politics: From the Colonial Period to the Present*, 2nd ed., ed. Mark A. Noll and Luke Harlow (New York: Oxford University Press, 2007), 269–95.

1965 . . . , the year Watts exploded and the Vietnam War escalated, when the reforms of the Voting Rights Act of 1965 and Immigration Act of 1965 were made law, the year when Vatican II concluded and decades of sustained growth in mainline Protestant church membership reversed. The . . . change in American congregations is apparent to the byways traveler: the mushrooming of conservative Protestant congregations and the disappearance of mainline ones. . . . The shift is obvious in small towns all across America, whose outskirts are strewn with brand-new wood-frame houses of worship and adjoining parking lots for the local Assemblies, Kingdom Halls, and Mormon wards, and whose stately brick downtown Presbyterian and Congregational churches have been merged or recycled as community museums and professional office buildings.[28]

The fact that white evangelicals have been growing proportionately at the same time that they have moved decisively into the Republican column explains the general significance of race-connected changes in this one constituency. Where evangelical Protestants made up only 24% of Richard Nixon's total vote in 1960, by 2004 they had come to make up 40% of George W. Bush's total (see table 5.3). The other significant conclusion to be drawn from examining the presidential vote coalitions is that changes in evangelical voting allegiance that began in the 1960s were matched by significant changes in other religious constituencies, and in none so obviously as among Roman Catholics.

RACE!

The Redirection of Catholic Voting

The Catholic contribution to the nation's recent political history turns on what the church has brought to national public life and on how national public life has affected the church. Catholics existed as a discernible, and increasingly significant, political force from the 1830s and the surge of immigration from traditionally Catholic parts of Europe.[29] Generally considered, that force had been exercised on behalf of the Democratic Party in its efforts to preserve local liberties against, first, Puritan-leaning Federalists, then the improvement-minded Whig Party, and then the WASP-guided Republicans.[30] Beginning with Franklin Roosevelt, leading Democrats rewarded Catholic political loyalty with increasing opportunities for significant political counsel. Father John Ryan, who was known as "the Right Reverend New Dealer" because of his devotion to President Roosevelt, exemplified the deepening affinity of Catholics and Democrats that was apparent in the 1930s. Significantly,

what made for that affinity was Roosevelt's increasing willingness to use government authority to support older people
(social security), strengthen the bargaining power of workers (support for unions), cushion the shocks of the business cycle (aid to the unemployed), and intervene to guide
the economy—in other words, to restructure the economy
along corporatist lines. Especially since the 1891 promulga-
tion of Pope Leo XIII's encyclical, *Rerum Novarum*, Catholic social thought had been moving in the same direction
toward a human-centered conception of public policy that
steered between unfettered capitalism and totalizing socialism. In contrast to typical instincts of white evangelicals,
who inclined toward social positions defined in strongly
individual terms, Catholic instincts moved in a more communal direction.[31] In the age of FDR, the traditional adherence of Catholics to the Democratic Party broadened out
from reasons of political advantage to a deeper ideological
affinity.

As table 5.1 suggests, this affinity continued, with some
fluctuations, through the 1968 presidential election. The personal popularity of Dwight D. Eisenhower, as well as Eisenhower's leadership of the Western powers against "godless
communism," cut into Catholic preference for Democrats.
But the overwhelming support for John F. Kennedy in 1960,
as well as much higher than national support for Lyndon
Johnson in 1964 and Hubert Humphrey in 1968, showed
that Catholic preference for the liberal candidates in each
of these years' elections remained strong. Of course, the
very strong Catholic vote for Kennedy, as the nation's first
Catholic president, was widely noticed at the time. The fact
that the Kennedy election preceded by only a few years the
opening of the Second Vatican Council, which seemed to
betoken a general liberalization of the church, appeared to

anticipate an even stronger Catholic-Democratic affinity for the future.

Yet even with large Catholic majorities for Johnson (1964) and Humphrey (1968), there were straws in the wind that pointed toward other aspects of Catholic tradition and other reactions to American developments. In the 1964 Johnson election, Barry Goldwater's best returns in New York State came from heavily Catholic Staten Island, which, only three decades earlier, had led the nation in support for FDR.[32] In 1968, although Hubert Humphrey easily outpaced Richard Nixon among Catholic voters nationwide, Nixon's advisors felt they had made a dent among Catholics by emphasizing Republican opposition to school busing, Republican toughness on crime, and Republican willingness to support parochial schools.[33] By 1972, when Nixon won the same percentage of Catholic votes as he did nationally in his victory over George McGovern, the straws in the wind had become a gale.

Two bore with special weight on electoral politics. First was the particular effects of the civil rights movement on Catholic political allegiance. Second was the *Roe v. Wade* Supreme Court decision of 1973 on abortion rights.

Civil rights reforms affected Catholics differently from how they affected white Protestants. Almost all northern Catholic leaders, along with some in the South, supported government measures to enhance black civil rights; on issues of voting, schools, public accommodations, and equal employment, most lay Catholics went along. On housing and affirmative action in heavily Catholic trade unions, however, it was another matter entirely. The Catholic parishes of the urban North had become nearly sacred spaces through intense community efforts at consecrating churches, constructing parochial schools, and providing family and social

services. The communalism that on a large scale predisposed this religious tradition *in favor* of Franklin Roosevelt's
national policies predisposed it *against* efforts to integrate
the northern neighborhoods that family- and community-
oriented Catholics had created. When civil rights meant
ending whites-only voting registration, Catholics in general agreed, and some notable figures, like Father Theodore Hesburgh of the University of Notre Dame, took
the lead. When nuns, priests, and brothers in clerical garb
joined the March on Washington in 1963 and the Selma-to-
Montgomery march in 1965, or when Father James Groppi
spearheaded the drive for open housing in Milwaukee, the
Catholic interracialism of the church's leadership enjoyed
its finest hours. But to the Catholic faithful whose neighborhoods were being desegregated, whose schools were
imperiled by shifting housing patterns, and whose secure
parish lives were menaced by disruption, crime, and rapid
change, it was another story. At the height of Milwaukee's
racial conflict in 1967, a concerned layman from Philadelphia wrote in pained phrases to Father Groppi: "It is not
fair to shove people of another race down our throats. The
Archbishops, Bishops, priests, the president, Robert Kennedy, and other people advocating open housing sit in their
single homes and tell us who to live with. We are as good as
you are and when all the people I have mentioned live in the
middle of row houses with people of other races I will too."[34]
Similar sentiments lay behind strong Catholic resistance to
government enforced open housing, and then government-
mandated busing for racial integration, in Chicago, Detroit,
Boston, and many other urban centers.

The convictions expressed in the letter to Father Groppi
registered a political turning point. Not race per se, but racial reform involving the disruption of cherished community

life, became a spark that blew up the seemingly permanent alliance of Catholic voters and national Democratic candidates. In John McGreevy's insightful words: "The many issues surrounding 'race' upset traditional political calculations. In retrospect, the emergence of 'race' as a partisan political issue in the 1960s—with conservative Republicans staking out positions on crime, welfare, busing, and affirmative action distinct from the positions of liberal Republicans as well as northern Democrats—proved to be a central political development of the postwar era."[35] Religion-related political change growing out of the circumstances of civil rights reform were reconfiguring the urban North as well as the white South.

Race, however, was not alone for Catholics, just as race was not alone for many white evangelicals. The Catholic communalism that gravitated toward large-government Democratic policies was also a communalism of traditional marriage and family. When *Roe v. Wade* arrived hard on the heels of civil rights reform, the political shocks were magnified. The Catholic tilt to political liberalism was not destroyed by the Supreme Court's abortion rights decision. Letters by the Catholic Bishops Conference on nuclear arms (1983) and the economy (1986) expressed enough confidence in politically liberal elements of Catholic social teaching to precipitate a neoconservative Catholic reaction that would come to include former civil rights liberals like Michael Novak and Richard John Neuhaus.

But alongside these liberal-leaning tendencies came also a great strengthening of conservative sentiments. The election of a Polish pope in 1978 shifted the dynamics of American Catholic politics, since John Paul II's anticommunist and morally traditional stances exerted a conservative influence from abroad. Perhaps even more, reaction against sexual revolution, gay rights advocacy, radical feminism, and, above all, *Roe v. Wade* pushed the Catholic hierarchy more and more into the political picture. Peter Steinfels has well described the consequences:

> Beginning in 1976, every presidential election became the occasion for a delicate episcopal dance. Candidates were pressed on their support for an anti-abortion measure like the Human Life Amendment; then individual bishops of varying prominence within the hierarchy signaled degrees of satisfaction or disappointment on this point while either stressing abortion as the all-important issue or rejecting single-issue voting—all the while trying to hew to their traditional position of not endorsing candidates.[36]

complicated

This dance, as Steinfels explains, grew increasingly partisan when, in response to their own core constituencies, Democrats became more uniformly pro-choice and Republicans moved strongly toward pro-life.

As with white evangelicals, Catholic political history was never lock-step. Even with the large changes of recent decades, loyalty to the Democratic Party remains strong among Catholics. Catholics still try to provide leadership that cuts across the grain of the standard U.S. ideological divisions—as illustrated by Cardinal Joseph Bernandin's promotion of a "seamless garment" of pro-life causes that took in both anti-abortion and anti-capital punishment. As for white evangelicals, so with Catholics: demographic, geographic, educational, economic, and regional factors have influenced political choices. Yet perceived over time, the recent history is still one of significant repositioning: in 1960 fewer than 20% of the nation's Catholics self-identified as Republicans, while more than 70% self-identified as

Democrats. In 2004 self-identification was almost even, at one-third for each party among Catholics who were active in their parishes (while Democrats retained a 32% to 28% edge among those not as active).[37] For the purposes of this book, it is significant that the alteration began in the 1960s, and that the wedge from which other things flowed was civil rights reform.

Observations

For both evangelicals and Catholics, it is necessary to specify carefully the place that reaction to civil rights reforms has occupied in recent political history. Among many evangelicals, primarily in the South, and among some Catholics, primarily in the North, race was the key matter pushing allegiance toward the Republican Party. Moreover, it was often an understanding of racial dynamics strongly shaped by deeply ingrained religious connections. But among Catholics and evangelicals, there have also been far larger numbers whose religion moved them to accept the government-mandated expansion of civil rights or at least not to contest that expansion. To the extent that such individuals have participated in the move to the Republican Party, race has not been the major factor, though other matters related to race in the unfolding of American history have often played a role. And for still others—many Catholics and some evangelicals—religious convictions positively required active commitment to civil rights. Where individuals with those convictions became Republican voters, it was usually despite strong commitments to civil rights. Without denying that a racial backlash against civil rights motivated some Catholics and evangelicals to vote Republican, and to do so for religious reasons, the far larger story is that civil rights precipitated other influences that drove political realignment.

Just as it is important to discern with care the place of religion in electoral behavior, so it is important to exercise the same care in accounting for broad political alignments. The relative success of the civil rights movement in ending enforced segregation in the South may be considered the opening that allowed "natural" political instincts finally to overcome the "artificial" results of the Civil War. So long as religion-backed white supremacy prevailed in the South—so long as Democratic allegiance in the South was protected by resentment against Republicans for "the war of northern aggression"—it was impossible for the small-government and largely Protestant ideology of white southerners to make common political cause with the small-government and substantially Protestant ideology of northern and western Republicans. After implementation of the civil rights legislation of 1964, 1965, and 1968, however, those reasons for separating ideologically small-government and largely Protestant political forces were much reduced. As James Nuechterlein has perceptively observed, the national civil rights legislation that the white South so vehemently opposed had an ironic effect: the white South "was thereby liberated, against its will, from the iron bond of race and freed, for the first time since the Civil War, to develop something like a normal politics, a politics where it was no longer unthinkable for whites to change party allegiance.... The move into the Republican Party was made possible by racial politics, but, once begun, had many other sources to perpetuate it."[38] After civil rights reforms took effect, the long-standing but informal Congressional alliance of southern Democrats and northern Republicans could evolve naturally into a national political alliance.

The key to blocking national civil rights had been a coalition of southern Democrats and congressional Republicans—southern Democrats for racist reasons, Republicans for small-government reasons. But so long as southern Democrats were defined as white racists, there was no possibility of realignment with the Republican Party, which no matter how much it championed small-government principles remained the party of Lincoln. Once legally enforced racism was out of the picture, however, it was much easier for the Republican Party to mount an appeal in the white South. Once segregation was gone, the promotion of a political agenda that championed personal responsibility, traditional values, and Judeo-Christian morality—in exploratory fashion by Barry Goldwater in 1964, with great effect by Ronald Reagan in 1980 and 1984, and with sustaining force by George Bush and Karl Rove in 2000 and 2004—enjoyed a broad national appeal, except in those parts of the country where other political goals had become more important.[39]

For African-American religion and politics, equal care is required to assess the results of the civil rights movement. Activistic Christianity was a powerful engine behind the movement, but expressed in a variety of forms and supported by significant nonreligious factors as well. From whatever perspective, however, it is clear that successful African-American mobilization for civil rights has not been the same as effective achievement of African-American civil society. Since the 1950s, the rapid growth in the black middle classes, the rapid increase of professional training, the beginning of fuller participation in government, and other significant gains have marked the nation's African-American population. But as a distinguished chorus of black leaders have consistently underscored, the achievements of the civil rights era represented a most important beginning, but a beginning requiring much additional moral, economic, and political effort to exploit. For the nation as a whole, and for African Americans in particular, the genuine gains of civil rights have not translated easily into an equitable society. Bitter complaints about the continuing effects of white racism on civil rights are well-known; they are often deserved. Less well known is the steady drumbeat of African-American injunctions aimed at African Americans to overcome the burdens of the "Black exceptional tradition" (Cornel West), to insist upon "Black Moral Self-Criticism" (Cheryl Sanders), to "covenant" for African-American moral discipline to match African-American political protest (Tavis Smiley), or to throw off "the Culture of Failure" that inhibits "Black America" (Juan Williams).[40]

An analogy is not far-fetched between white evangelical Protestant exertions in the antebellum period and black Christian exertions in the civil rights era. Just as evangelical religion decisively shaped national culture in that earlier era, so too did the reforming Christianity of African Americans decisively shape the nation's life in the decades after World War II. Yet just as the national culture shaped by evangelical religion faltered when it moved beyond culture-formation to confront the conflict over slavery, so the political nation redirected by the civil rights movement has not yet successfully addressed the economic, social, moral, and educational problems of a society persistently divided between black and white. As in the earlier era, when the religious achievements (and failures) were national, as well as southern and northern, so too in recent U.S. history have the religious achievements (and failures) been national, as well as black and white.

In an address from November 2004, the former governor of Mississippi, William F. Winter, offered a sobering reflection on the deep South, but one that could also be applied to the nation as a whole: "I must tell you that the problem of race, despite all the progress that we have made, remains the thorniest, trickiest and most difficult barrier that we confront to achieve a truly successful and united region."[41] From 1619, when the first African indentured servants were offloaded in the American colonies, until the 1960s, American political institutions wavered in deciding whether African Americans could be full and equal citizens of a democratic nation. Since that time, the nation's laws have made this commitment, though whether laws are enough remains in question. A general principle of American democracy demands that members of every race and ethnic group be treated equally before the law, but a general fact of history demands that sustained, accumulated wrongs must be addressed by sustained, ongoing remediation. The most chilling words ever spoken about the fruits of American inequality were part of the second inaugural address of Abraham Lincoln, in March 1865: "Yet if God wills that it [the Civil War] continue, until all the wealth piled by the bond-man's two hundred and fifty years of unrequited toil shall be sunk, and until every drop of blood drawn with the lash, shall be paid with another drawn with the sword, as was said three thousands years ago, so still it must be said 'the judgments of the Lord are true and righteous altogether.'" Lincoln's keen awareness was that especially a people who repeatedly call on the name of the Lord place themselves under the highest possible standard for defining good and evil.

Shortly after Lincoln made this speech, the Civil War did come to an end. Yet the "scourge," the "offense," of race-defined social inequality did not end until much later, if in fact it has actually come to an end. The United States pays a heavy price, and it pays it daily, for its history of injustice to African-American citizens. African Americans who wait for redress, who do not take into their own hands the challenge of shaping the future, compound this larger difficulty. The dilemmas that result from the nation's history demand painstaking moral reasoning, since they involve the ultimately important questions of divine will and human responsibility. Somewhat more simple are the contingent realities of history: race in connection with religion has decisively shaped the nation's political history, as, in various forms and through various means, it continues to do.

Theological Conclusion

A sensible historian would now end with a summary, as follows. I have set out what I think is a coherent interpretation of American political history from the 1820s to the present: the Civil War solved the religion and slavery problem, but it did not solve the religion and race problem. Neither did Reconstruction nor the national and regional arrangements that followed Reconstruction. To the extent that the race and religion problem has ever been solved in American life, it began to be addressed only after World War II when an aggressive expression of African-American religion was met by a federal government willing to exert broad national authority on behalf of civil rights. But this exertion of central authority was much stronger than American republican sympathies had ever before been asked to countenance. And even with unprecedented levels of national federal action, the recent past has only begun to address the problems of race that continue to bedevil the nation. Moreover, if the combination of black religious self-assertion and broad governmental action led to genuine progress in some aspects of civil rights, it also led to a significant political conflict, especially when white evangelical Christians and some Roman Catholics, even as they accommodated themselves to black civil rights, mobilized for political action because of offense at the expansion of governmental authority.

At this point my historical summary is complete. But because the events and situations I have described are so deeply interwoven into the fabric of all American history and are also so profoundly moral in their implications, I am prompted to move beyond historical interpretation to a broader conclusion that responds to the central dilemma posed by this history. That dilemma starts with a positive judgment: the American political tradition has been in many ways exemplary for its morality as well as for its ideological cogency and economic efficiency. Among the strongest elements in the ideology of American democratic republicanism is the fear of overweening excesses of unchecked central government authority. In my judgment, this fear is well grounded. Concentrations of centralized government power have—time and again, at home and abroad—infringed liberties, violated principles of subsidiarity, encouraged tyranny by unrepresentative and unelected experts, and needlessly sabotaged vibrant local traditions. Moreover, the American practice of republican democracy has, in fact, worked out for the betterment of great numbers for more than two hundred years. It is, on balance, a humane, enlightened, and good system; comparatively speaking, it is among the best political systems ever witnessed in human history. In addition, the Christian faith that has been so prominent in so many ways throughout American history has, again on balance, been a beneficent force at home and abroad. Christian altruism, Christian philanthropy, Christian consolation, and Christian responsibility are not the only forces for good in American history, but they loom very large and have had very positive effects.

And yet . . . and yet . . . . The American political system and the American practice of Christianity, which have provided so much good for so many people for so many years, have never been able to overcome race. In 1971 one of Walker Percy's characters expressed the difficulty dramatically in Percy's novel *Love in the Ruins*, and in my view he got it right:

> Was it the nigger business from the beginning? What a bad joke: God saying, here it is, the new Eden, and it is yours because you're the apple of my eye, because you the lordly Westerners, the fierce Caucasian-Gentile-Visigoths, believed in me and in the outlandish Jewish Event even though you were nowhere near it and had to hear the news of it from strangers. But you believed and so I gave it all to you, gave you Israel and Greece and science and art and the lordship of the earth, and finally even gave you the new world that I blessed for you. And all you had to do was pass one little test, which was surely child's play for you because you had already passed the big one. One little test: here's a helpless man in Africa, all you had to do is not violate him. That's all.
>
> One little test: you flunk!
>
> God, was it always the nigger business, now, just as in 1883, 1783, 1683, and hasn't it always been that ever since the first tough God-believing Christ-haunted cunning violent rapacious Visigoth-Western-Gentile first set foot here with the first black man . . . ?[1]

The conundrum that Walker Percy phrased so forcefully as a religious question requires at least an effort at religious explanation.

For the American history of race and religion, which has had such a manifest impact on American politics, only a complex interpretation can suffice. To explain the simultaneous manifestation of superlative good and pervasive malevolence in this history of race and religion, neither simple trust in human nature nor simple cynicism about American hypocrisy is adequate. Economic and geographical interpretations, interpretations that feature the exercise of dominion by some people over others, or those that stress the innate human longing for freedom actually do illuminate much in American history. But by themselves they do not have the capacity to explain paradoxical behaviors that coexist within the same historical framework. An example is provided by Erskine Clarke's splendid book *Dwelling Place: A Plantation Epic*, where similar beliefs in God as divine sovereign are shown to have made the white family of Charles Colcock Jones simultaneously more altruistic in domestic, political, and economic duties and more efficient in exploiting their slaves, while roughly the same beliefs made the extended black family of Lizzy Jones simultaneously more accommodating to their lot as slaves and more psychologically self-reliant.[2]

Others may offer persuasive explanations to account for what has been so thoroughly commingled in the American history of race, religion, and politics. That commingling has included domination with liberation, false consciousness with genuine idealism, altruism with greed, self-seeking with self-sacrifice, economic independence with economic exploitation, tribalism with universalism, hatred with love. Any final explanation for the conundrums of American history must be able to account for a mind-stretching conjunction of opposites. It must evoke both the goodness of the human creation and the persistence of evil in all branches of humanity. It must bring together the reality of humans transformed by good and the incompleteness of all such transformations. It must show how the best human creatures are sabotaged by their own hubris and the worst human depredations are enlightened by unexpected shafts of light. It must bring together the reality of evil in those whom we most admire and the reality of good in those whom we most despise. And it must be able to hold these contradictions, antinomies, and paradoxes in one cohesive vision.

Throughout American history, what I have called the broad Calvinist tradition has been responsible for many of the achievements, but also many of the problems, that require a consideration of contradictions, antinomies, and paradoxes. Most obviously, reliance on the Bible has produced spectacular liberation alongside spectacular oppression. Yet from the much used and much abused Scriptures, a long line of Christian readers have affirmed in varying accents and diverse emphases a transcendent account of profound complexity to take the measure of human nature and human achievement.

Details would be different for Leonard Bacon, Henry McNeal Turner, Francis Grimké, William Jennings Bryan, Reinhold Niebuhr, or Fannie Lou Hamer. But the outline of convictions would be similar: God made humans, and the creation was good—yet at the same time, humankind is fallen and will never escape the effects of sin. Further, God offers in the work of his Son, Jesus Christ, and in the power of his Holy Spirit, the transforming prospect of redemption—yet redemption never equals perfection; the redeemed must always recognize their own shortcomings and be filled with gratitude for all the gifts of creation, including all other human creatures. Ultimately, because the manifestation of God in Jesus Christ is, at the same time, so thoroughly human and so thoroughly divine, so completely infinite and so completely finite, the heart of the Christian faith offers the hint of an explanation for how the commingling of contradictions, antinomies, and paradoxes can occur in other spheres of life.

The history of American race, religion, and politics from Nat Turner to George W. Bush is a narrative in which contradictions, antimonies, and paradoxes abound. For making sense of this tangled history it is helpful to proceed from a standpoint with a scope for moral complexity as wide as the heights of goodness and depths of evil within that history. Historic Christian faith offers such a standpoint from which it is possible to see how much believers themselves have done to promote the evils of racism in American politics while at the same time recognizing how often they have offered hints of redemption as well.

Notes

INTRODUCTION

1. For a well-chosen selection of such views, see Milton B. Powell, ed., *The Voluntary Church: American Religious Life, 1740–1860, Seen through the Eyes of European Visitors* (New York: Macmillan, 1967).

2. Barnet Schecter, *The Devil's Own Work: The Civil War Draft Riots and the Fight to Reconstruct America* (New York: Wagner, 2005), 242–43.

3. Paul Joseph Münz, "Christentum und Sklaverei," *Historisch-politische Blätter für das katholische Deutschland* 62 (1868): 180, 202.

4. Michael Kazin, *A Godly Hero: The Life of William Jennings Bryan* (New York: Knopf, 2006), 161.

5. Information on presidential elections is from *Presidential Elections, 1789–2000* (Washington, D.C.: CQ Press, 2002).

6. Francis J. Grimké, "Discouragements: Hostility of the Press[,] Silence and Cowardice of the Pulpit," in *The Works of Francis J. Grimké*, vol. 1: *Addresses Mainly Personal and Racial*, ed. Carter G. Woodson, (Washington, D.C.: Association Publishers, 1942), 237–38 (his text was Ps. 27:14—"Wait on the Lord; be of good courage, and He shall strengthen thine heart"). I thank Thabiti Anyabwile for bringing these works of Grimké to my attention.

7. Grimké, "Sources from Which no Help May Be Expected,—The General Government, Political Parties," in ibid., 256 (text: also Ps. 27:14).

8. This paragraph and the next two depend on Taylor Branch, *Pillar of Fire: America in the King Years, 1963–65* (New York: Simon and Schuster, 1998), 592–94, 597–99.

9. Andrew Kohut, ed., *Trends 2005* (Washington, D.C.: Pew Research Center, 2005), 35. Similar proportions for 2000 are reported by John Green and Mark Silk, "The New Religious Gap," special supplement, *Religion in the News* 6, 3 (Fall 2003): 1–3, 15.

10. "Special Report: American Election," *Economist*, January 31, 2004, 24.

11. *The Civil War as a Theological Crisis* (Chapel Hill: University of North Carolina Press, 2006). In chapters 1 and 3 below I adapt and abridge some material from this book, as well as from *America's God: From Jonathan Edwards to Abraham Lincoln* (New York: Oxford University Press, 2002), in setting the stage for what follows.

12. David L. Chappell, *A Stone of Hope: Prophetic Religion and the Death of Jim Crow* (Chapel Hill: University of North Carolina Press, 2004).

13. Some of that work has been published as Dennis C. Dickerson, "African American Religious Intellectuals and the Theological Foundations of the Civil Rights Movement, 1930–55," *Church History* 74 (June 2005): 217–35; and Thabiti Anyabwile, *The Decline of African American Theology: From Biblical Faith to Cultural Captivity* (Downers Grove, Ill.: InterVarsity Press, 2007).

14. Michael Fellman, Lesley J. Gordon, and Daniel E. Sutherland, *This Terrible War: The Civil War and Its Aftermath* (New York: Pearson Education, 2003).

15. Taylor Branch, *Parting the Waters: America in the King Years, 1954–63* (New York: Simon and Schuster, 1988); *Pillar of Fire*; and *At Canaan's Edge: America in the King Years, 1965–68* (New York: Simon and Schuster, 2006).

CHAPTER ONE: *The Bible, Slavery, and the "Irrepressible Conflict"*

1. Well-selected samples are found in Davis W. Houck and David E. Dixon, eds., *Rhetoric, Religion, and the Civil Rights Movement, 1954–1965* (Waco: Baylor University Press, 2006); and Mason I. Lowance, Jr., *A House Divided: The Antebellum Slave Debates in America, 1776–1865* (Princeton: Princeton University Press, 2003), 88–115.

2. All election information, except where otherwise noted, is from *Presidential Elections, 1789–2000* (Washington, D.C.: CQ Press, 2002).

3. For South Carolina, popular voting for president began only in 1868; for Alabama, there was no federal election in 1864.

4. In 1860 the Democratic percentages are calculated by combining the totals for the national Democratic candidate (Stephen A. Douglas) and the southern Democratic candidate (John C. Breckinridge). In 1924 the Democratic totals combine the vote for Democratic John W. Davis and Progressive Robert M. La Follette. For 1948 the Democratic totals combine votes for the Democrat Harry S. Truman and the Dixiecrat J. Strom Thurmond.

5. With this procedure, however, proportions in the figure become quite large if the national Democratic vote is very small, as in Republican

landslide years; similarly, the proportions for all states are pulled lower in Democratic landslide years.

6. Anne Farrow, Joel Lang, and Jenifer Frank, *Complicity: How the North Promoted, Prolonged, and Profited from Slavery* (New York: Ballantine Books, 2005).

7. Leon F. Litwack, *North of Slavery: The Free States, 1790–1860* (Chicago: University of Chicago Press, 1961). For one of the very rare exceptions to this general rule, see the story of Covert, Michigan, which was peacefully and thoroughly integrated from the mid-1860s, as related in Anna-Lisa Cox, *A Stronger Kinship: One Town's Extraordinary Story of Hope and Faith* (New York: Little, Brown, 2006).

8. For a long-standing northern practice of excluding African Americans from some towns and cities, see James E. Loewen, *Sundown Towns: A Hidden Dimension of American Racism* (New York: New Press, 2005).

9. See especially Daniel Walker Howe, *The Political Culture of the American Whigs* (Chicago: University of Chicago Press, 1979).

10. For strong statements arguing for the centrality of slavery in the constitutional era and the early national period, see Paul Finkelman, "Slavery and the Constitutional Convention: Making a Covenant with Death," in *Beyond Confederation: Origins of the Constitution and American National identity*, ed. Richard R. Beeman et al. (Chapel Hill: University of North Carolina Press, 1986); Robin L. Einhorn, *American Taxation, American Slavery* (Chicago: University of Chicago Press, 2006); and Matthew Mason, *Slavery and Politics in the Early American Republic* (Chapel Hill: University of North Carolina Press, 2006). For a rejoinder concerning at least some of the conclusions drawn by these historians, see Don E. Fehrenbacher, *The Slaveholding Republic: An Account of the United States Government's Relation to Slavery* (New York: Oxford University Press, 2001).

11. David Brion Davis, "Part Three: Expanding the Republic, 1820–1860," in *The Great Republic: A History of the American People* (Lexington, Mass.: D. C. Heath, 1977), 1:588.

12. André Siegfried, *America Comes of Age: A French Analysis* (New York: Harcourt, Brace, 1927), 34.

13. W. Fred Graham, *The Constructive Revolutionary: John Calvin and His Socio-Economic Impact* (Atlanta: John Knox, 1971), 21.

14. This theme is well developed in Peter R. D'Agostino, *Rome in America: Transnational Catholic Ideology from the Risorgimento to Fascism* (Chapel Hill: University of North Carolina Press, 2004).

15. Siegfried, *America Comes of Age*, 35.

16. See Thomas J. Curry, *The First Freedoms: Church and State in America to the Passage of the First Amendment* (New York: Oxford University Press, 1986).

17. Jefferson to James Smith, December 8, 1822, in *Jefferson's Extracts from the Gospels*, ed. Dickinson W. Adams, *The Papers of Thomas Jefferson, Second Series* (Princeton: Princeton University Press, 1983), 409

18. See Nathan O. Hatch, *The Democratization of American Christianity* (New Haven: Yale University Press, 1989).

19. Elizabeth Fox-Genovese and Eugene D. Genovese, *The Mind of the Master Class: History and Faith in the Southern Slaveholders' Worldview* (New York: Cambridge University Press, 2005), 80.

20. David Walker, *Appeal in Four Articles; Together with a Preamble, to the Coloured Citizens of the World, but in Particular, and Very Expressly, to Those of the United States of America*, ed. Charles M. Wiltse (New York: Hill and Wang, 1965), 42.

21. See Herbert Aptheker, *Nat Turner's Slave Rebellion* (New York: Humanities, 1966); Kenneth S. Greenberg, ed., *Nat Turner: A Slave Rebellion in History and Memory* (New York: Oxford University Press, 2003).

22. For that distinction, see Robert Bruce Mullin, "Biblical Critics and the Battle over Slavery," *Journal of Presbyterian History* 61 (1983): 210–26.

23. Charles Grandison Finney, *Lectures on Revivals of Religion* (1835), ed. William G. McLoughlin (Cambridge, Mass.: Harvard University Press, 1960), 301, 302.

24. See Donald G. Mathews, *Religion in the Old South* (Chicago: University of Chicago Press, 1977).

25. For a fuller summary and extensive literature, see Mark A. Noll, *The Civil War as a Theological Crisis* (Chapel Hill: University of North Carolina Press, 2006), 31–50.

26. Leonard Bacon, *Slavery Discussed in Occasional Essays, from 1833 to 1846* (New York: Baker and Scribner, 1846), 180. Emphasis added.

27. Alexis de Tocqueville, *Democracy in America*, ed. and trans. Harvey C. Mansfield and Debra Winthrop (Chicago: University of Chicago Press, 2000), 278–80.

28. C. C. Goen, *Broken Churches, Broken Nation: Denominational Schisms and the Coming of the Civil War* (Macon, Ga.: Mercer University Press, 1985); Richard A. Carwardine, *Evangelicals and Politics in Antebellum America* (New Haven: Yale University Press, 1993).

29. Richard K. Crallé, ed., *The Works of John C. Calhoun*, vol. 4: *Speeches of John C. Calhoun, Delivered in the House of Representatives and the Senate of the United States* (New York: Appleton, 1854), 557–58.

30. The material in this paragraph summarizes Mark A. Noll, *America's God: From Jonathan Edwards to Abraham Lincoln* (New York: Oxford University Press, 2002), 161–86.

31. Nathan Bangs, *A History of the Methodist Episcopal Church*, 4 vols. (New York: T. Mason and G. Lane, 1839), 1:46.

32. The underappreciated links between these revivals and the gathering crisis over slavery have been well treated in Kathryn T. Long, *The Revival of 1857–58: Interpreting an American Religious Awakening* (New York: Oxford University Press, 1998).

33. This section summarizes Noll, *The Civil War as a Theological Crisis*, 51–74.

34. Daniel Alexander Payne, *Welcome to the Ransomed; or, Duties of the Colored Inhabitants of the District of Columbia* (Baltimore: Bull and Tuttle, 1861), 10–11; as collected in Payne, *Sermons and Addresses, 1853–1891*, ed. Charles Killian (New York: Arno, 1972). Emphasis added.

35. Fox-Genovese and Genovese, *The Mind of the Master Class*.

36. Philip Schaff, "Slavery and the Bible," *Mercersburg Review* 13 (April 1861): 316–17; emphasis in original.

37. John G. Fee, *The Sinfulness of Slaveholding Shown by Appeals to Reason and Scripture* (New York: John A. Gray, 1851), 29, 28. For a careful introduction to Fee's milieu, see Luke E. Harlow, "Antislavery Clergy in Antebellum Kentucky, 1830–1860" (M.A. thesis, Wheaton College, 2004).

38. "Speech at Cincinnati, Ohio," September 17, 1859, in *The Collected Works of Abraham Lincoln*, ed. Ray P. Basler, 9 vols. (New Brunswick, N.J.: Rutgers University Press, 1953), 3:445.

39. Frederick Douglass, "The Pro-Slavery Mob and the Pro-Slavery Ministry," *Douglass' Monthly*, March 1861, 417–18.

40. "Traveling Preacher, No. 3," *Christian Index*, August 31, 1837, as quoted in Kenneth Startup, "'A Mere Calculation of Profits and Loss': The Southern Clergy and the Economic Culture of the Antebellum North," in *God and Mammon: Protestants, Money, and the Market, 1790–1860*, ed. Mark A. Noll (New York: Oxford University Press, 2002), 220. Startup's fuller treatment of such conjunctions is found in his book, *The Root of All Evil: The Protestant Clergy and the Economic Mind of the Old South* (Athens: University of Georgia Press, 1997).

41. Fox-Genovese and Genovese, *Mind of the Master Class*, 526.

42. Douglass quoted in Harry S. Stout, *Upon the Altar of the Nation: A Moral History of the Civil War* (New York: Viking, 2006), 184.

43. Quoted in ibid., 384.

44. C. C. Gillespie, "The Confederate Motto, No Compromise," *Army and Navy Messenger for the Trans-Mississippi Department*, March 16,

2, as quoted in Kurt O. Berends, "'Thus Saith the Lord,' the Use of the Bible by Southern Evangelicals in the Era of the American Civil War" (Ph.D. diss., Oxford University, 1997), 235.

45. Joseph Edmund Jörg, "Der Wendepunkt," *Historisch-politische Blätter für das katholische Deutschland* 51 (1863): 237.

46. James M. McPherson, *For Cause and Comrades: Why Men Fought in the Civil War* (New York: Oxford University Press, 1997), 63. For a fine general survey, see Robert J. Miller, *Both Prayed to the Same God: Religion and Faith in the American Civil War* (Lanham, Md.: Lexington, 2007).

47. James M. McPherson, "Afterword," in *Religion and the American Civil War*, ed. Randall M. Miller, Harry S. Stout, and Charles Reagan Wilson (New York: Oxford University Press, 1998), 412.

48. Stout, *Upon the Altar of the Nation*, 213

49. Ibid., 405.

50. David W. Blight, *Race and Reunion: The Civil War in American Memory* (Cambridge, Mass.: Harvard University Press, 2006).

CHAPTER TWO: *The Origins of African-American Religious Agency*

1. I draw especially on Daniel W. Stowell, *Rebuilding Zion: The Religious Reconstruction of the South, 1863–1877* (New York: Oxford University Press, 1998), 80–99, 130–45; with outstanding general background provided by John Hope Franklin, *From Slavery to Freedom: A History of Negro Americans*, 5th ed. (New York: Knopf, 1980), 227–50.

2. See especially Michele Mitchell, *Righteous Propagation: African Americans and the Politics of Racial Destiny after Reconstruction* (Chapel Hill: University of North Carolina Press, 2004).

3. Eric Foner, *Reconstruction, 1863–1877: America's Unfinished Revolution* (New York: Harper and Row, 1988), 88.

4. For a recent account of Allen's work, see Wallace D. Best, "Richard Allen and the Rise of Bethel African Methodist Episcopal Church, Part I and Part II," *AME Church Review* 120 (January–March 2004): 25–52; and 120 (April–June 2004): 18–39.

5. See Albert J. Raboteau, *Slave Religion: The "Invisible Institution" in the Antebellum South*, 2nd ed. (New York: Oxford University Press, 2004); and Sylvia R. Frey and Betty Wood, *Come Shouting to Zion: African American Protestantism in the American South and British Caribbean* (Chapel Hill: University of North Carolina Press, 1998).

6. Daniel Alexander Payne, *Recollections of Seventy Years* (New York: Arno, 1968 [1888], 256.

7. See Thabiti Anyabwile, *The Decline of African American Theology: From Biblical Faith to Cultural Captivity* (Downers Grove, Ill.: InterVarsity Press, 2007), 114–15.

8. Quoted in ibid., 117–18.

9. Francis J. Grimké, "Evangelism and Institutes of Evangelism," in *The Works of Francis J. Grimké*, vol. 1: *Addresses Mainly Personal and Racial*, ed. Carter G. Woodson (Washington, D.C.: Association Publishers, 1942), 523–24.

10. Quoted in Stephen Ward Angell, *Bishop Henry McNeal Turner and African-American Religion in the South* (Knoxville: University of Tennessee Press, 1992), 256.

11. A solid review of internal African-American debates, along with a poignant account of how much the nation's racist regime hamstrung all black reforming efforts of the era, is found in David Sehat, "The Civilizing Mission of Booker T. Washington," *Journal of Southern History* 73 (May 2007): 323–62.

12. See note 5 above, as well as Eugene D. Genovese, *Roll, Jordan, Roll: The World the Slaves Made* (New York: Pantheon, 1974); and Paul Harvey, *Freedom's Coming: Religious Culture and the Shaping of the South from the Civil War through the Civil Rights Era* (Chapel Hill: University of North Carolina Press, 2005).

13. W.E.B. DuBois, *The Souls of Black Folk* (Boston: Paperview/Boston Globe, 2005 [1903]), 137, 139, 138.

14. See Danielle Brune Sigler, "Beyond the Binary: Revisiting Father Divine, Daddy Grace, and Their Ministries," in *Race, Nation, and Religion in the Americas*, ed. Henry Goldschmidt and Elizabeth McAlister (New York: Oxford University Press, 2004), 209–27.

15. Stephen A. Marini, "The Government of God: Religion and Revival in America, 1764–1792," ms.

16. Pauline Hopkins, *Contending Forces: A Romance Illustrative of Negro Life North and South* (1900), as quoted in Kathleen Clark, "Future Generations," *Reviews in American History* 35 (2005): 203.

17. W.E.B. DuBois, "The Niagara Movement: Declaration of Principles, 1905," in *Pamphlets and Leaflets by W.E.B. DuBois*, ed. Herbert Aptheker (White Plains, N.Y.: Kraus-Thomson, 1986), 57–58.

18. For other accounts that stress in different ways how African Americans were strengthened by the nation's racist regime prevailing after the 1870s, see Evelyn Brooks Higginbotham, *Righteous Discontent: The Women's Movement in the Black Baptist Church* (Cambridge, Mass.: Harvard University Press, 1993); Steven Hahn, *A Nation under Our Feet: Black Political Struggles in the Rural South from Slavery to the Great Migration*

(Cambridge: Harvard University Press, 2003); and Nan Woodruff, *American Congo: The African-American Struggle for Freedom in the Delta* (Cambridge, Mass.: Harvard University Press, 2003).

CHAPTER THREE: *The Churches, "Redemption," and Jim Crow*

1. "Farewell Address" (September 19, 1796), in *Washington: Writings* (New York: Library of America, 1997), 971.

2. See Gaines M. Foster, *Moral Reconstruction: Christian Lobbyists and Federal Legislation of Morality, 1865–1920* (Chapel Hill: University of North Carolina Press, 2002).

3. The next paragraphs put to use what I have written in *The Civil War as a Theological Crisis* (Chapel Hill: University of North Carolina Press, 2006), 8, 159–60.

4. See Elisha Mulford, *The Republic of God* (Boston: Houghton Mifflin, 1881); and Josiah Strong, *Our Country: Its Possible Future and Its Present Crisis* (New York: Baker and Taylor, 1885). For discussion, see Foster, *Moral Reconstruction*; and John T. McGreevy, *Catholicism and American Freedom* (New York: Norton, 2003). I thank Bryan Bademan for help on this point.

5. See Sally Barringer Gordon, *The Mormon Question: Polygamy and Constitutional Conflict in Nineteenth-Century America* (Chapel Hill: University of North Carolina Press, 2002); and Kathleen Flake, *The Politics of American Religious Identity: The Seating of Senator Reed Smoot, Mormon Apostle* (Chapel Hill: University of North Carolina Press, 2004).

6. My understanding of these matters has been influenced especially by Michael Fellman, Lesley J. Gordon, and Daniel E. Sutherland, *This Terrible War: The Civil War and Its Aftermath* (New York: Longman, 2003); Eric Foner, *Reconstruction: America's Unfinished Revolution, 1863 to 1877* (New York: Harper and Row, 1988); Eric Foner and Joshua Brown, *Forever Free: The Story of Emancipation and Reconstruction* (New York: Knopf, 2005); and John Hope Franklin, *Reconstruction after the Civil War*, 2nd ed. (Chicago: University of Chicago Press, 1994).

7. For a recent rendering of this northern story, see David Quigley, *Second Founding: New York City, Reconstruction, and the Making of American Democracy* (New York: Hill and Wang, 2004), with 100–104 on Greeley's ideological evolution.

8. I am following the excellent account by Nicholas Lemann, *Redemption: The Last Battle of the Civil War* (New York: Farrar, Straus and Giroux, 2006).

9. Quoted in ibid., 69.

10. Ibid., xi.

11. For outstanding examples, see W. Fitzhugh Brundage, *Lynching in the New South: Georgia and Virginia, 1880–1930* (Urbana: University of Illinois Press, 1993); and Donald G. Mathews, "Lynching Is Part of the Religion of Our People: Faith in the Christian South," in *Religion in the American South: Protestants and Others in History and Culture*, ed. Beth Barton Schweiger and Donald G. Mathews (Chapel Hill: University of North Carolina Press, 2004), 153–94.

12. Christopher Hill, *Society and Puritanism in Pre-Revolutionary England* (New York: Schocken, 1964).

13. These include Daniel W. Stowell, *Rebuilding Zion: The Religious Reconstruction of the South, 1863–1877* (New York: Oxford University Press, 1998); James B. Bennett, *Religion and the Rise of Jim Crow in New Orleans* (Princeton: Princeton University Press, 2005); Edward J. Blum, *Reforging the White Republic: Race, Religion, and American Nationalism, 1865–1898* (Baton Rouge: Louisiana State University Press, 2005); Paul Harvey, *Freedom's Coming: Religious Culture and the Shaping of the South from the Civil War through the Civil Rights Era* (Chapel Hill: University of North Carolina Press, 2005); and Edward J. Blum and W. Scott Poole, eds., *Vale of Tears: New Essays on Religion and Reconstruction* (Macon, Ga.: Mercer University Press, 2005). These new studies build on solid older works like Charles Reagan Wilson, *Baptized in Blood: The Religion of the Lost Cause, 1865 to 1920* (Athens: University of Georgia Press, 1980); and Gaines M. Foster, *Ghosts of the Confederacy: Defeat, the Lost Cause, and the Emergence of the New South, 1865 to 1913* (New York: Oxford University Press, 1987).

14. Kimberly R. Kellison, "Parameters of Promiscuity: Sexuality, Violence, and Religion in Upcountry South Carolina," in *Vale of Tears*, 25.

15. Lemann, *Redemption*, 45.

16. This account follows Darren E. Grem, "Sam Jones, Sam Hose, and the Theology of Racial Violence," *Georgia Historical Quarterly* 90 (2006): 35–61.

17. I am following Blum, *Reforging the White Republic*.

18. Lyle W. Dorsett, *A Passion for Souls: The Life of D. L. Moody* (Chicago: Moody Press, 1997), 111, 126, 246.

19. Blum, *Reforging the White Republic*, 91–95.

20. Ibid., 98–103.

21. Ibid., 198–208.

22. Horace Bushnell, "Our Obligations to the Dead," in *Building Eras in Religion* (New York, 1881), 328–29.

23. At this point, I am following Harry S. Stout, *Upon the Altar of the Nation: A Moral History of the Civil War* (New York: Viking, 2006).

24. David W. Blight, *Race and Reunion: The Civil War in American Memory* (Cambridge, Mass.: Harvard University Press, 2006), with, as noted above (chap. 1, n. 6), an occasional exception as in Covert, Michigan.

25. The argument is sketched in Michael Phillips's discussion of the dispensationalist C. I. Schofield's career as an influential Bible teacher in Dallas; see Phillips, *White Metropolis: Race, Ethnicity, and Religion in Dallas, 1841–2001* (Austin: University of Texas Press, 2006). The connection is not far-fetched, as illustrated by the fraternal connections of A. C. Dixon (1854–1925), an influential fundamentalist pastor and opponent of the Social Gospel, and Thomas Dixon (1864–1946), a playwright and novelist whose works like *The Clansman* offered a racist depiction of Reconstruction and "the new South."

26. See especially Douglas Frank, *Less Than Conquerors: How Evangelicals Entered the Twentieth Century* (Grand Rapids: Eerdmans, 1986).

27. Michael Kazin, *A Godly Hero: The Life of William Jennings Bryan* (New York: Knopf, 2006), 162.

28. On Douglass, see the helpful account in Ralph Luker, *The Social Gospel in Black and White* (Chapel Hill: University of North Carolina Press, 1991), 301–10.

29. See Christopher H. Evans, *The Kingdom Is Always but Coming: A Life of Walter Rauschenbusch* (Grand Rapids: Eerdmans, 2004), 253–56; and for general background, Ronald White, *Liberty and Justice for All*, rev. ed. (Louisville: Westminster John Knox, 2002).

30. The next paragraphs follow the well-documented interpretation of Michael Hochgeschwender, *Wahrheit, Einheit, Ordnung: Die Sklavenfrage und der amerikanische Katholizismus, 1835–1870* (Paderborn: Ferdinand Schöningh, 2006). For further insight on this neglected topic, see John T. McGreevy, "Catholics and Abolition: A Historical (and Theological) Problem," in *Figures in the Carpet: Finding the Human Person in the American Past*, ed. Wilfred McClay (Grand Rapids: Eerdmans, 2007), 405–27.

31. Hochgeschwender, *Wahrheit, Einheit, Ordnung*, 425.

32. Bennett, *Religion and the Rise of Jim Crow in New Orleans*; and "Catholics, Creoles, and the Redefinition of Race in New Orleans," in *Race, Nation, and Religion in the Americas*, ed. Henry Goldschmidt and Elizabeth McAlister (New York: Oxford University Press, 2004), 183–208.

33. Hammon, "An Evening Thought," in Sandra A. O'Neale, *Jupiter Hammon and the Biblical Beginnings of African-American Literature* (Metuchen, N.J.: Scarecrow, 1993), 59.

34. I have this quotation from George A. Rawlyk.

35. Edwin Scott Gaustad and Philip L. Barlow, *New Historical Atlas of Religion in America* (New York: Oxford University Press, 2001), 376–81, sec. C.17.

36. Kazin, *A Godly Hero*, 147.

37. Blight, *Race and Reunion*; Stout, *Upon the Altar of the Nation*.

38. I thank Christopher Luse of Emory University for helpful orientation on this subject.

39. Reginald Horsman, *Josiah Nott of Mobile: Southerner, Physician, and Racial Theorist* (Baton Rouge: Louisiana State University Press, 1987); and George M. Fredrickson, *The Black Image in the White Mind: The Debate on the Afro-American Character and Destiny, 1817–1914* (New York: Harper and Row, 1971).

40. See David N. Livingstone, *Adam's Ancestors: Race, Religion, and the Politics of Human Origins* (Baltimore: Johns Hopkins University Press, 2008); and George M. Fredrickson, *Racism: A Short History* (Princeton: Princeton University Press, 2002), 51–67.

41. For more on the waxing and waning of deference to Scripture, see Eugene D. Genovese, *A Consuming Fire: The Fall of the Confederacy in the Mind of the White Christian South* (Athens: University of Georgia Press, 1998).

42. In sorting out the history of civil rights jurisprudence after the Civil War, I am grateful for the assistance provided by David Noll.

43. Ervin Chemerinksy, *Constitutional Law: Principles and Policies*, 3rd ed. (New York: Aspen, 2006), 494–97.

44. Fellman, Gordon, and Sutherland, *This Terrible War*, 516.

45. Chemerinksy, *Constitutional Law*, 507–8.

46. 163 U.S. 537 (1896); quoted from http://supreme.justia.com/us/163/537/case.html (April 12, 2007); for necessary context, see Linda Przybyszewski, *The Republic According to John Marshall Harlan* (Chapel Hill: University of North Carolina Press, 1999), 2, 95–100, and passim.

47. 189 U.S. 475 (1903); quoted from http://supreme.justia.com/us/189/475/case.htm (April 12, 2007).

48. Jennifer Snow, "The Civilization of White Men: The Race of the Hindu in *United States v. Bhagat Singh Thind*," in *Race, Nation, and Religion*, 259–82.

CHAPTER FOUR: *Religion and the Civil Rights Movement*

1. Norman H. Clark, *Deliver Us from Evil: An Interpretation of American Prohibition* (New York: Norton, 1976), remains a convincing account.

2. For strong race-religion influences in this 1928 election, see Glenn Feldman, "Home and Hearth: Women, the Klan, Conservative Religion, and Traditional Family Values," in *Politics and Religion in the White South*, ed. Glenn Feldman (Lexington: University Press of Kentucky, 2005), 72–78. The ratios are figured as the percentage of the Democratic

candidate's percentage of the state vote divided by the candidate's percentage of the national vote.

3. Nancy J. Weiss, *Farewell to the Party of Lincoln: Black Politics in the Age of FDR* (Princeton: Princeton University Press, 1983), 217–20 (quotations on 220).

4. David L. Chappell, *A Stone of Hope: Prophetic Religion and the Death of Jim Crow* (Chapel Hill: University of North Carolina Press, 2004), 4.

5. For an outstanding collection of speeches, from whites as well as blacks, elites and nonelites, that reflects the diversity of tributaries flowing into civil rights thinking, see Davis W. Houck and David E. Dixon, eds., *Rhetoric, Religion, and the Civil Rights Movement* (Waco: Baylor University Press, 2006).

6. Branch, *Parting the Waters*, 74.

7. Ibid., 90–92.

8. For examples of Niebuhr's views, see *Moral Man and Immoral Society* (New York: Scribner's, 1932), 252–56; and *The Children of Light and the Children of Darkness* (New York: Scribner's, 1944), 139–42; and for discussion, Chappell, *A Stone of Hope*, 26–66.

9. Branch, *At Canaan's Edge*, 578–79.

10. See especially Dennis Dickerson, "African American Religious Intellectuals and the Theological Foundations of the Civil Rights Movement, 1930–55," *Church History* 74 (June 2005): 217–35, which offers an excellent introduction to the individuals and sources I draw on for the paragraphs that follow. On this subject, I also benefited greatly from a panel made up of Dennis Dickerson, Walter Fluker, Randall Jelks, and David Chappell on "The Religious Origins of the Civil Rights Movement," American Society of Church History (Philadelphia), January 7, 2006. For further treatment of several black religious figures, as well as an excellent introductory survey of the history of African-American religious thought, see Clarence Taylor, *Black Religious Intellectuals: The Fight for Equality from Jim Crow to the Twenty-First Century* (New York: Routledge, 2002).

11. See Richard I. McKinney, *Mordecai, the Man and His Message: The Story of Mordecai Wyatt Johnson* (Washington, D.C.: Howard University Press, 1997).

12. Benjamin Elijah Mays and Joseph William Nicholson, *The Negro's Church* (New York: Institute of Social and Religious Research, 1933), 288.

13. Richard I. McKinney, *Religion in Higher Education among Negroes* (New Haven: Yale University Press, 1945), 135.

14. Howard Thurman, *Jesus and the Disinherited* (New York: Abingdon-Cokesbury, 1949), 14–15.

15. William Stuart Nelson, *The Christian Way in Race Relations* (New York: Harper and Brothers, 1947), viii.

16. Benjamin Mays, "The Obligations of Individual Christians," in ibid., 224.

17. George D. Kelsey, "The Christian Way in Race Relations," in ibid., 47–48.

18. For a succinct restatement of this thesis, see Chappel, *A Stone of Hope*, 186–87.

19. Charles M. Payne, *I've God the Light of Freedom: The Organizing Tradition and the Mississippi Freedom Struggle* (Berkeley: University of California Press, 1995), 274.

20. Ibid., 309.

21. Charles Marsh, *God's Long Summer: Stories of Faith and Civil Rights* (Princeton: Princeton University Press, 1997), 13–24 and passim.

22. Payne, *I've God the Light of Freedom*, 309.

23. Branch, *At Canaan's Edge*, 321.

24. On Tindley and also this particular composition, see Robert Darden, *People Get Ready! A New History of Black Gospel Music* (New York: Continuum, 2004), 160–63.

25. For excellent contextual work on African-American appropriation of Scripture, which blossomed during the civil rights era, see Vincent L. Wimbush and Rosamond C. Rodman, eds., *African Americans and the Bible: Sacred Texts and Social Textures* (New York: Continuum, 2000); and Allan Dwight Callahan, *The Talking Book: African Americans and the Bible* (New Haven: Yale University Press, 2006).

26. Branch, *Parting the Waters*, 525, 542.

27. The list is taken from ibid., passim; Branch, *Pillar of Fire*, passim; and *At Canaan's Edge*, passim.

28. On the significant enhancement of federal judicial reach for one array of cases, which dates from the 1940s, see James Hitchcock, *The Supreme Court and Religion in American Life*, vol. 1: *The Odyssey of the Religion Clauses* (Princeton: Princeton University Press, 2004), 60–89.

29. For a perceptive discussion, see John Witte, Jr., *Religion and the American Constitutional Experiment*, 2nd ed. (Boulder: Westview, 2005), 136–38, 152–55, 251–52.

30. For this judgment, along with dissent to it, see John F. Wilson and Donald L. Drakeman, *Church and State in American History*, 3rd ed. (Boulder: Westview, 2003), 201–6. An energetic debate over whether Jefferson was merely making a political statement for the moment or was attempting to set out a principle for all time is found in the symposium, James H. Hutson, et al., "Thomas Jefferson's Letter to the Danbury

Baptists: a Controversy Rejoined," *William & Mary Quarterly* 56 (October 1999): 775–824.

31. *Historical Statistics of the United States: Colonial Times to 1957* (Washington, D.C.: U.S. Bureau of the Census, 1960), 491.

32. For a narrative about civil rights that features economic conditions and responses to them, see Jacquelyn Dowd Hall, "The Long Civil Rights Movement and the Political Uses of the Past," *Journal of American History* 91 (March 2005): 1233–63.

33. On the latter, see Wallace D. Best, *Passionately Human, No Less Divine: Religion and Culture in Black Chicago, 1915–1952* (Princeton: Princeton University Press, 2005).

34. For a wide-ranging literature exploring economic change in connection with the growth of suburbs and recent political history, see the extensive notes in Hall, "The Long Civil Rights Movement"; and also the solid studies by Kevin M. Kruse, *White Flight: Atlanta and the Making of Modern Conservatism* (Princeton: Princeton University Press, 2005); Matthew D. Lassiter, *The Silent Majority: Suburban Politics in the Sunbelt South* (Princeton: Princeton University Press, 2006); and Joseph Crespino, *In Search of Another Country: Mississippi and the Conservative Counterrevolution* (Princeton: Princeton University Press, 2007).

35. See especially Mary L. Dudziak, *Cold War Civil Rights: Race and the Image of American Democracy* (Princeton: Princeton University Press, 2000).

36. For how these phrases came to enjoy official status, see Henry J. Cadbury, "In God We Trust," *Christian Century*, July 7, 1954, 822; Nat Brandt, "To the Flag," *American Heritage*, June 1971, 72–104; and National Legal Foundation, "In God We Trust," www.nlf.net/in_god_we_trust. htm (October 28, 2002).

37. Perceptive reviews include John M. Giggie, *Reviews in American History* 33 (2005): 254–62; Randall Jelks, *Church History* 73 (December 2004): 828–33; and Paul Harvey, *North Star* 7 (Spring 2004), northstar.vassar.edu/volume7/chappell.html.

38. For more on this subject, see the section "The Redirection of Catholic Voting" in chapter 5.

39. Joel A. Carpenter, *Revive Us Again: The Reawakening of American Fundamentalism* (New York: Oxford University Press, 1997).

40. Chappell, *A Stone of Hope*, 107–8.

41. D. Bruce Lockerbie, "Introduction" to Frank E. Gaebelein, *The Christian, the Arts, and Truth* (Portland, Ore. Multnomah, 1985), 44.

42. L. Nelson Bell, "An Important Statement: An Appeal to Fellow Christians," *Southern Presbyterian Journal*, April 11, 1956, 8; as quoted in Michael D. Hammond, "Conscience in Crisis: Neo-evangelicals and Race in the 1950s" (M.A. thesis, Wheaton College, 2002), 55.

43. Chappell, *A Stone of Hope*, 96–97, 140–44. See also the careful account by Steven P. Miller, "Billy Graham, Civil Rights, and the Changing Postwar South," in *Politics and Religion in the White South*, 157–86; and the insightful discussion of race in Andrew Finstuen, "The Prophet and the Evangelist: The Public 'Conversation' of Reinhold Niebuhr and Billy Graham," *Books & Culture*, July/August 2006, 8–9, 37–42.

44. Chappell, *A Stone of Hope*, 117–21, 140–43.

45. The best critique of this argument that I have read is J. Russell Hawkins, "Southern Religion in Massive Resistance" (seminar paper, Rice University, 2006), but there is also solid material in Clive Webb, "Introduction," and Jane Dailey, "The Theology of Massive Resistance: Sex, Segregation, and the Sacred after Brown," in *Massive Resistance: Southern Opposition to the Second Reconstruction*, ed. Clive Webb (New York: Oxford University Press, 2005), 3–17 and 151–80; Jane Dailey, "Sex, Segregation, and the Sacred after Brown," *Journal of American History* 91 (June 2004): 119–44; and several of the chapters in Feldman, *Politics and Religion in the White South*.

46. See the section "Religious Factors in the Divide over Slavery" in chapter 1.

47. For deep background, see David M. Goldenberg, *The Curse of Ham: Race and Slavery in Early Judaism, Christianity, and Islam* (Princeton: Princeton University Press, 2003); and for a reflective essay on this book that brings considerations closer to the present, David Brion Davis, "Blacks: Damned by the Bible," *New York Review of Books*, November 16, 2006, 37–40.

48. On the religious motives of Sam Bowers of the Klan, see Marsh, *God's Long Summer*, 53–81.

49. Mark Newman, *Getting Right with God: Southern Baptists and Desegregation, 1945–1995* (Tuscaloosa: University of Alabama Press, 2001); Wayne Flynt, *Alabama Baptists: Southern Baptists in the Heart of Dixie* (Tuscaloosa: University of Alabama Press, 1998), 455–516.

50. Newman, *Getting Right with God*, 60, 84.

CHAPTER FIVE: *The Civil Rights Movement as the Fulcrum of Recent Political History*

1. The following paragraph draws on Mark A. Noll, "Introduction," in *Religion and American Politics: From the Colonial Period to the Present*, ed. Mark Noll and Luke Harlow, 2nd ed. (New York: Oxford University Press, 2007).

2. As a partial list, see Randall Balmer, *Thy Kingdom Come: How the Religious Right Distorts the Faith and Threatens America: An Evangelical Lament*

(New York: Basic Books, 2006); Greg Boyd, *The Myth of a Christian Nation: How the Quest for Political Power Is Destroying the Church* (Grand Rapids: Zondervan, 2006); Mark Ellingsen, *When Did Jesus Become Republican? Rescuing Christianity from the Right* (Lanham, Md.: Rowman and Littlefield, 2007); Michael Feldman, *Divided by God: America's Church-State Problem—and What We Should Do about It* (New York: Farrar, Straus, and Giroux, 2005); Michelle Goldberg, *Kingdom Coming: The Rise of Christian Nationalism* (New York: Norton, 2006); David Ray Griffin et al., *American Empire and the Commonwealth of God: A Political, Economic, and Religious Statement* (Louisville: Westminster John Knox, 2006); Sam Harris, *Letter to a Christian Nation* (New York: Knopf, 2006); George G. Hunter III, *Christian, Evangelical, and . . . Democrat?* (Nashville: Abingdon, 2006); Patrick Hynes, *In Defense of the Religious Right: Why Conservative Christians Are the Life-blood of the Republican Party and Why That Terrifies the Democrats* (Nashville: Nelson Current, 2006); Jan G. Linn, *Big Christianity: What's Right with the Religious Left* (Louisville: Westminster John Knox, 2006); Charles Marsh, *Wayward Christian Soldiers: Against the Political Captivity of the Gospel* (New York: Oxford University Press, 2007); Kevin Phillips, *American Theocracy: The Peril and Politics of Radical Religion, Oil, and Borrowed Money in the 21st Century* (New York: Viking, 2006); Mark Toulouse, *God in Politics: Four Ways American Christianity and Politics Relate* (Louisville: Westminster/John Knox, 2007); Jim Wallis, *God's Politics: Why the Right Gets It Wrong and the Left Doesn't Get It* (San Francisco: HarperSanFrancisco, 2005); and Mel White, *Religion Gone Bad: The Hidden Dangers of the Religious Right* (New York: Penguin/Tarcher, 2006).

3. Again, as only samples, see Monique El-Faizy, *God and Country: How Evangelicals Become America's Mainstream* (New York: Bloomsbury, 2006); Nancy Gibbs and Michael Duffy, *The Preacher and the Presidents: Billy Graham in the White House* (New York: Center Street, 2007); Richard Kyle, *Evangelicalism: An Americanized Christianity* (New Brunswick, N.J.: Transaction Books, 2006); D. Michael Lindsay, *Faith in the Halls of Power: How Evangelicals Joined the American Elite* (New York: Oxford University Press, 2007); Lauren Sandler, *Righteous: Dispatches from the Evangelical Youth Movement* (New York: Viking, 2006); and Jeffrey L. Sheler, *Believers: A Journey into Evangelical America* (New York: Viking Penguin, 2006).

4. For examples, see Dean C. Coddington and Richard L. Chapman, *God Bless America: Patriotic Fervor or Historic Reality?* (New York: iUniverse, 2006); David L. Holmes, *The Faiths of the Founding Fathers* (New York: Oxford University Press, 2006); James Hutson, ed., *The Founders on Religion: A Book of Quotations* (Princeton: Princeton University Press, 2005); Isaac Kramnick and R. Laurence Moore, *The Godless Constitution: A Moral*

Defense of the Secular State, 2nd ed. (New York: Norton, 2005); Jon Meacham, *American Gospel: God, the Founding Fathers, and the Making of a Nation* (New York: Random House, 2006); James P. Moore, Jr., *One Nation Under God: The History of Prayer in America* (New York: Doubleday, 2005); Noll and Harlow, *Religion and American Politics*; Michael Novak and Jana Novak, *Washington's God* (New York: Basic Books, 2006); Donald W. Shriver, *Honest Patriots: Loving a Country Enough to Remember Its Misdeeds* (New York: Oxford University Press, 2005); Gary Scott Smith, *Faith and the Presidency: From George Washington to George W. Bush* (New York: Oxford University Press, 2006); Thomas Wang, ed., *America, Return to God* (Sunnyvale, Ca.: Great Commission Center International, 2006); and Garry Wills, *Head and Heart: American Christianities* (New York: Penguin, 2007).

5. Among the best are the works cited in chapter 4, note 34, along with Darren Dochuk, "From Bible Belt to Sunbelt: Plain Folk Religion, Grassroots Politics, and the Southernization of Southern California, 1939–1969" (Ph.D. diss., University of Notre Dame, 2005); Glenn Feldman, ed., *Politics and Religion in the White South* (Lexington: University Press of Kentucky, 2005); Michael O. Emerson and Christian Smith, *Divided by Race: Evangelical Religion and the Problem of Race in America* (New York: Oxford University Press, 2000); and several essays in both Beth Barton Schweiger and Donald G. Mathews, eds., *Religion in the American South; Protestants and Others in History and Culture* (Chapel Hill: University of North Carolina Press, 2004); and Clive Webb, ed., *Massive Resistance: Southern Opposition to the Second Reconstruction* (New York: Oxford University Press, 2005).

6. For example, Earl Black and Merle Black, *The Rise of Southern Republicans* (Cambridge, Mass.: Harvard University Press, 2002); William E. Leuchtenberg, *The White House Looks South: Franklin D. Roosevelt, Harry S. Truman, Lyndon B. Johnson* (Baton Rouge: Louisiana State University Press, 2005); and two books by James M. Glaser, *Race, Campaign Politics, and the Realignment of the South* (New Haven: Yale University Press, 1996), and *The Hand of the Past in Contemporary Southern Politics* (New Haven: Yale University Press, 2005).

7. John A. Kirk, "'Massive Resistance and Minimum Compliance': The Origins of the 1957 Little Rock School Crisis and the Failure of School Desegregation in the South," in *Massive Resistance,* 76–98.

8. Branch, *Parting the Waters,* 823–24.

9. An excellent chronology can be found in Tavis Smiley, ed., *The Covenant in Action* (Carlsbad, Ca.: Smiley Books, 2006), 101–74.

10. Kevin M. Kruse, *White Flight: Atlanta and the Making of Modern Conservatism* (Princeton: Princeton University Press, 2005), 206.

11. A rapidly growing literature now exists on connections between civil rights and evangelical political mobilization. Excellent accounts of ongoing debates generated by that literature are provided in two essay reviews by David L. Chappell, "Civil Rights: Grassroots, High Politics, or Both?" *Reviews in American History* 32 (2004): 565–72; and "Did Racists Create the Suburban Nation?" ibid. 35 (2007): 89–97. This theme is also prominent in most of the titles referenced in notes 2 through 5 of this chapter.

12. I have benefited especially from Klaus P. Fischer, *America in White, Black, and Gray: The Stormy Sixties* (New York: Continuum, 2006); Philip Jenkins, *Decade of Nightmares: The End of the Sixties and the Making of Eighties America* (New York: Oxford University Press, 2006); Mark Oppenheimer, *Knocking on Heaven's Door: American Religion in the Age of Countercultures* (New Haven: Yale University Press, 2003); the relevant sections of Patrick Allitt, *Religion in America since 1945* (New York: Columbia University Press, 2003); and, extending the chronology only slightly, Natasha Zaretsky, *No Direction Home: The American Family and the Fear of National Decline, 1968–1980* (Chapel Hill: University of North Carolina Press, 2007).

13. *Presidential Elections, 1789–2000* (Washington, D.C.: CQ Press, 2002), 147–48.

14. The quoted phrases here are from Branch, *At Canaan's Edge*, passim, but they can be found in any historical account of the period.

15. The paragraphs that follow draw on works mentioned in notes 5 and 6 for this chapter, as well as Branch, *Parting the Waters*; *Pillar of Fire*; and *At Canaan's Edge*.

16. Branch, *Pillar of Fire*, 494–96.

17. See David John Marley, "Riding the Back of the Bus: The Christian Right's Adoption of Civil Rights Movement Rhetoric," in *The Civil Rights Movement in United States Memory*, ed. Renee Christine Romeno and Leigh Raiford (Athens: University of Georgia Press, 2006).

18. Branch, *At Canaan's Edge*, 542.

19. Kruse, *White Flight*, 15.

20. Nick Kotz, *Judgment Days: Lyndon Baines Johnson, Martin Luther King, Jr., and the Laws That Changed America* (Boston: Houghton Mifflin, 2005), 154.

21. William A. Mueller, "Current Religious Thought," *Christianity Today*, February 18, 1957, 39 (support for Supreme Court); E. Earle Ellis, "Segregation and the Kingdom of God," ibid., March 18, 1957, 6–9 (defense); Editorial, "The Church and the Race Problem," ibid., March 18, 1957, 20–22; and the letters column, April 15, 1957, 24–25.

22. See Dochuk, "From Bible Belt to Sunbelt"; and "Evangelicalism Becomes Southern, Politics Becomes Evangelical: From FDR to Ronald Reagan," in *Religion and American Politics*, 297–325.

23. Robert Wuthnow, *The Restructuring of American Religion: Society and Faith since World War II* (Princeton: Princeton University Press, 1988).

24. See Ronald L. Numbers, *The Creationists*, 2nd ed. (Cambridge, Mass.: Harvard University Press, 2006); and James R. Moore, "Interpreting the New Creationism," *Michigan Quarterly Review* 22 (1983): 321–34.

25. See Barry Hankins, *Francis Schaeffer: Fundamentalist Warrior, Evangelical Prophet* (Grand Rapids: Eerdmans, 2008).

26. Donald G. Mathews and Jane Sherron De Hart, *Sex, Gender, and the Politics of ERA: A State and the Nation* (New York: Oxford University Press, 1990), 173.

27. For a cautious, well-grounded presentation of evidence, see David E. Campbell and J. Quin Monson, "The Case of Bush's Reelection: Did Gay Marriage Do It?" in *A Matter of Faith: Religion in the 2004 Presidential Election*, ed. David E. Campbell (Washington: Brookings Institution Press, 2007), 120–41. Their conclusion is that the gay marriage issue probably helped Bush, but not enough to justify the conclusion that it was *the* central factor in his victory.

28. R. Stephen Warner, "The Place of the Congregation in the Contemporary Religious Configuration" (orig. published 1994), in Warner, *A Church of Our Own: Disestablishment and Diversity in American Religion* (New Brunswick: Rutgers University Press, 2005), 147.

29. For an excellent survey, see James Hennessey, S.J., "Roman Catholics and American Politics, 1900–1960," in *Religion and American Politics*, 247–65.

30. See the section "Among Catholics" in chapter 3.

31. For the evangelicals, see Emerson and Smith, *Divided by Race*; and Michael O. Emerson and Rusty Hawkins, "Viewed in Black and White: Conservative Protestantism, Racial Issues, and Oppositional Politics," in *Religion and American Politics*, 327–43. For the Catholics, see John T. McGreevy, *Catholicism and American Freedom* (New York: Norton, 2003).

32. John T. McGreevy, *Parish Boundaries: The Catholic Encounter with Race in the Twentieth-Century Urban North* (Chicago: University of Chicago Press, 1996), 195. This entire section depends heavily on the insights of *Parish Boundaries*.

33. Ibid., 234.

34. Quoted in ibid., 204.

35. Ibid., 194.

36. Peter Steinfels, "Roman Catholics and American Politics, 1960–2004," in *Religion and American Politics*, 354.

37. Luis Lugo, ed., *Religion and Public Life: A Faith-Based Partisan Divide* (Washington, D.C.: Pew Research Center, 2005), 7, 15.

38. James Nuechterlein, "How Race Wrecked Liberalism," *First Things*, August/September 2005, 35.

39. This insight is well developed in Feldman, ed., *Politics and Religion in the White South*. For expert treatment of religious factors in the 2004 election, see Campbell, ed., *A Matter of Faith*.

40. Cornel West, *Prophecy Deliverance! An African-American Revolutionary Christianity* (Louisville: Westminster John Knox, 1987); Cheryl Sanders, *Empowerment Ethics for a Liberated People* (Minneapolis: Fortress, 1995); Tavis Smiley, ed., *The Covenant with Black America* (Chicago: Third World Press, 2006); Juan Williams, *Enough: The Phony Leaders, Dead-End Movements, and Culture of Failure That Are Undermining Black America—and What We Can Do about It* (New York: Crown, 2006).

41. Quoted in David S. Broder, "Mississippi Healing," *Washington Post*, January 16, 2005, B7. The paragraph that follows modifies Mark A. Noll, "Voting Not To Vote," in *One Electorate under God? A Dialogue on Religion and American Politics*, ed. E. J. Dionne, Jr., Jean Bethke Elshtain, and Kayla M. Drogosz (Washington, D.C.: Brookings Institution Press, 2004), 155–558.

THEOLOGICAL CONCLUSION

1. Walker Percy, *Love in the Ruins* (New York: Picador, 1971), 57.

2. Erskine Clarke, *Dwelling Place: A Plantation Epic* (New Haven: Yale University Press, 2005).

Index

Great Society, 124, 146, 147. *See also*
  Johnson, Lyndon
Greeley, Horace, 71
Gregory XVI, Pope, 83
Grem, Darren, 191n16
Grimké, Francis, 5, 9, 53, 59, 180
Groppi, James, 167

Hahn, Steven, 189n18
Hall, Jacquelyn Dowd, 196nn32 and
  34
Ham, curse of, 133
Hamer, Fannie Lou, 116, 133, 180
Hamilton, Alexander, 62
Hammon, Jupiter, 85–86
Hammond, Michael, 196n42
Harlan, John, 98
Harlow, Luke, 187n37
Hatch, Nathan, 186n18
Hawkins, J. Russell, 197n45, 201n31
Hayes, Rutherford B., 73
Hennesey, James, 201n29
Hesburgh, Theodore, 167
Higginbotham, Evelyn Brooks, 189n18
Higher Education Act (1965), 147
Hill, Christopher, 74–75
Hitchcock, James, 195n28
Hochgeschwender, Michael, 84,
  192nn30 and 31
Holmes, Oliver Wendell, 99
Hopkins, Pauline, 58, 59
Hose, Sam, 76
Houk, David, 184n1, 194n5
Howard, O. O., 77
Howe, Daniel Walker, 185n9
Human Life Amendment, 169
Humphrey, Hubert, 165, 166
Hutson, James, 195–96n30

Immigration Reform Bill (1965), 147,
  163
Irish-Americans, 3–4, 82, 84

Jackson, Andrew, 17, 21, 22, 61
Jackson, Jimmy Lee, 7, 8, 9
Jefferson, Thomas, 21, 29, 61, 125

Jim Crow laws, 58, 81, 82, 85, 89, 94,
  113
John Paul II, Pope, 168
Johnson, Andrew, 68
Johnson, Lyndon, 8, 124, 147, 149,
  165, 166; and civil rights legislation,
  117–18, 140–41, 153. *See also* Great
  Society
Johnson, Moredecai W., 109
Jones, C. P., 50
Jones, Charles Colcock, 179
Jones, Lizzy, 179
Jones, Sam, 76, 77

Kazin, Michael, 93
Kelsey, George D., 109, 113, 114
Kennedy, D. James, 157
Kennedy, John F., 104, 126, 139, 140,
  147, 165, 167
Kerry, John, 9, 136
King, Martin Luther Jr., 107, 117,
  118, 138, 139, 140; religious
  thought of, 108–9, 113–14
King, Rodney, 20
Knights of the White Camelia, 76
Kruse, Kevin, 141, 152, 196n34
Ku Klux Klan, 76, 84, 97

Lamar, L.C.Q., 72
Lassiter, Mathew, 196n34
Lee, Cager, 7
Lemann, Nicholas, 72, 190n8
Leo XIII, Pope, 165
Lincoln, Abraham, 40, 45, 84, 172,
  174, 175
Little Rock, Arkansas, 138
Livingstone, David, 193n40
Loewen, James, 185n8
Long, Kathryn, 187n32
Louisiana, in Reconstruction, 84–85
Lovejoy, Elijah, 37
Lowance, Mason, 184n1
Luker, Ralph, 192n28
Luse, Christopher, 193n38
Luther, Martin, 25–26
Lutherans, 25–26, 87